BFI TV Classics

BFI TV Classics is a series of books celebrating key individual television programmes and series. Television scholars, critics and novelists provide critical readings underpinned with careful research, alongside a personal response to the programme and a case for its 'classic' status.

Also Published:

Buffy the Vampire Slayer
Anne Billson

Doctor Who
Kim Newman

Edge of Darkness
John Caughie

The Office
Ben Walters

Our Friends in the North
Michael Eaton

Queer as Folk
Glyn Davis

Seinfeld
Nicholas Mirzoeff

Seven Up
Stella Bruzzi

The Singing Detective
Glen Creeber

The Likely
Lads

Phil
Wickham

A BFI book published by Palgrave Macmillan

© Phil Wickham 2008

First published in 2008 by
PALGRAVE MACMILLAN
Houndmills, Basingstoke, Hampshire RG21 6XS and
175 Fifth Avenue, New York, N.Y. 10010
Companies and Representatives throughout the world

on behalf of the

BRITISH FILM INSTITUTE
21 Stephen Street, London W1T 1LN
www.bfi.org.uk

There's more to discover about film and television through the BFI. Our
world-renowned archive, cinemas, festivals, films, publications and learning
resources are here to inspire you.

PALGRAVE MACMILLAN is the global academic imprint of the Palgrave Macmillan
division of St. Martin's Press, LLC and of Palgrave Macmillan Ltd.
Macmillan® is a registered trademark in the United States, United Kingdom
and other countries. Palgrave is a registered trademark in the European
Union and other countries.

Images from *The Likely Lads*, © BBC; pp. 36–7 – *Get Carter* © MGM; p. 82 – *Peep Show*
© Objective Productions/Channel 4.

Set by Cambrian Typesetters, Camberley, Surrey
Printed in China

This book is printed on paper suitable for recycling and made from fully
managed and sustained forest sources. Logging, pulping and manufacturing
processes are expected to conform to the environmental regulations of the
country of origin.

British Library Cataloguing-in-Publication Data
A catalogue record for this book is available from the British Library

ISBN 978–1–84457–213–7

Contents

Acknowledgments

Many thanks to all those who helped in the birth of this book: David McGowan and staff at the BBC Written Archive; Rebecca Barden and Sophie Contento at BFI Publishing; Steve Bryant at the BFI; Dick Clement and Ian La Frenais (of course), who were very generous with their time; and Ed Hanson.

Thanks also to those who helped me through it all: my mum and dad, who introduced me to Bob and Terry in the first place, and the rest of my family; Andy Salter (which of us is Terry and which of us is Bob?); Rebecca and Steve again; my wonderful friend Moira; Gaby Johnson; Bryony Dixon; and most of all to Helen.

Dedicated to the memory of
Moira Mooney (1963–2007)

Introduction

Sometime in the 1970s I became transfixed by a TV sitcom that my parents watched and loved. Our family had recently moved from the North to the South and it felt as if it spoke about our lives, our history. The show was *Whatever Happened to the Likely Lads?* (BBC 1973–4), and thirty years on my reaction to it is just as enthusiastic; it remains as funny as when I first saw it; more so as I have got older and had more of the experiences that it describes and can appreciate its truth and its subtlety.

Every time I hear the first bar of the theme tune I'm hooked again. It's a kind of folk-rock choral explosion bursting from the screen, as a male voice sings 'OOOoooh what happened to you, whatever happened to me?'. Black-and-white stills of two young men having fun together spring out from an image of a photo album as the singer asks 'What became of the people we used to be?'.

Suddenly, the pictures become colour and the screen splits into four squares. On the left are two images of brutalist municipal modernist architecture – multi-storey car parks, or perhaps a new shopping centre. On the bottom right is a long shot of a number of huge new tower blocks, the 'cities in the sky' dreamt of by council planning committees. In the top right square a confident, expensively couiffured, man, about thirty, strides out of a new house towards his car, keys in hand. He smiles at the camera, proud of his trappings of success.

The song continues, telling us 'Tomorrow's almost over, the days went by so fast'.

'Tomorrow's almost over, the days went by so fast'

'It's the only thing to look forward to – the past'

Four more squares appear on the screen. On the left are images of the Tyneside docks and a grim, Victorian industrial panorama of bridges. On the bottom left children are playing in the ruins of old terrace back-to-backs in the process of demolition. Through their windows we can just make out a sea of new tower blocks on the horizon. To the bottom right appears another youngish man, less smartly dressed. He holds a paper and attempts to hail an approaching bus on a terraced street. As it sails past him he turns to us and scowls, as the singer of our song informs us that 'It's the only thing to look forward to – the past'.

This opening credit sequence promises viewers so much – it tells us that this show will be dealing with some big questions about the new and the old, the past, the present and the future. The pictures, together with the words of the song, make it clear that this is a complex business, it's not just about a changing society but about the personal too; do we ever change? Can we? Should we? Do we want to?

Something about the men's faces, one plump and apparently self-satisfied, one tougher and looking thoroughly disgruntled, tell us that it will also be funny, that these questions will be probed through humour, laughing at the ironies of human nature.

The black-and-white photos that spring from the album are of the same young men we see in colour, but some years earlier; less lined and a bit more carefree. Some sort of history that we, the audience, might understand is implied here – we might have known these lads when these pictures were taken. Indeed many people did. As its name implies, *Whatever Happened to the Likely Lads?* is a follow-up to *The Likely Lads*, a show about these same two young men that was screened some years earlier, in black and white, between 1964 and 1966.

This gives another clue about the show. It relies on its viewers. It asks us about our memories of this older series featuring the same characters and invites connections with it, relating those two chirpy lads dressed the same and living the same kind of life to these men who now seem so different to each other. Likewise, I will suggest it offers a connection to the viewer, encouraging a reflexive mode of engagement,

3

so we might ask questions of ourselves, and think about our own memories and what they might mean.

TV programmes often form part of the fabric of our daily lives and we can develop a relationship with them, characters and situations edging their way into our consciousness until we know them as well as our family and friends. *Whatever Happened to the Likely Lads?* and *The Likely Lads* are about everyday life, the ordinary things that can happen, both each day and over the course of many years, about the thoughts and the feelings we have as we go about our routines. It's about going to work, getting married, going out for a pint, about standing still or deciding to move on or up, about what we keep and what we leave behind.

The everyday quality of TV and the way we use it makes it the perfect medium to consider and comment on the ordinary. TV has a multitude of forms, and crucially acres of time, in which to communicate with us and is able to do so directly in our own space. Some of these forms are particularly well placed to build up a relationship with us by introducing characters and situations we can understand and recognise. One is sitcom, where we are often encountering something that seems very much like real life, just with the amusing bits accentuated. Nothing seems 'unreal' about *Whatever Happened to the Likely Lads?* or about its chief protagonists Bob Ferris (the smart, confident one, played by Rodney Bewes) or Terry Collier (the scowling scruffy one played by James Bolam); they might remind many viewers of themselves or their friends. The situations they find themselves in are indeed 'likely' – it is the reactions to them and the character traits that make them react in that way that are funny and make us laugh, that and the howl of recognition of realising that it could happen to us.

I believe *Whatever Happened to the Likely Lads?* and its predecessor are classics and this book will attempt to show why. There's so much in there, it truly is a 'rich text'. For instance, the series considers working-class English culture at a key moment in its history. It also asks what it is to be a man; what is expected of you, and what are the terms of the relationship between men and women? I will explore what makes the show funny by looking at the nature of its comedy, especially through the writing of its authors, Dick Clement and Ian La Frenais. I interviewed both men in writing the book and I will use their comments to illuminate some of the points and to find out more about the history of the series.

Finally, I want to consider the crux of the show, the main reason why I think it's up there in the pantheon of greats. *Whatever Happened to the Likely Lads?* deals in ideas about time and failure and loss. Its humour is so funny because it dares to do this, because it recognises our dilemma, our condition and has the courage to make us think (and laugh) about it. It appeals to aspects of universal experience and this excites me about the programme. I understand that one has to be duly cautious in claiming universality I am not suggesting that literally everybody will understand the programme in this light or feel that way about regret, or ageing, or times past and, yes, there is much else about the programme that might seem specifically male, or Northern, or English, or working class. However, I think a lot of people watching might feel a connection with the feelings that Bob and Terry express, or suppress, and, furthermore, Clement and La Frenais quite explicitly encourage them to do so. Making connections to your own life from books, films, or TV shows can in some circumstances be painful, but it can also be intensely pleasurable and liberating – this is what I feel when watching *The Likely Lads* and I don't think I'm the only one.

Sometimes in writing about television one has, necessarily, to spend much time describing the intricacies of a series' narratives over many pages. In contrast the overarching storyline here can be described in two short paragraphs.

Two young lads in their early twenties, Bob Ferris and Terry Collier, work as electricians in a big factory on North Tyneside. They drink lots of beer, chase lots of girls and live for fun. Bob, the more ambitious of the two, decides to join the Army. Missing him, Terry joins up too, only to find Bob discharged for flat feet.

5

Five years later they meet again on a train as Terry is demobbed. Bob is shortly to be married to his girlfriend Thelma, a librarian with wealthy parents. Bob now works as a surveyor for Thelma's builder father and is planning a new young executive life on the Elm Lodge housing estate, having already become a stalwart of the badminton club. Terry, in contrast, rejects Bob's attempts to move up the social ladder and relishes remaining as an unreconstructed Northern working-class man, trying to recreate the lifestyle he left five years earlier. Bob is torn between his background and past with Terry and the brave new world ahead of him with Thelma.

It is not plot that is our interest in the show; it is character and situation, the place and the time, that gives meaning to those characters. This is not comedy that comes from funny costumes or surreal manifestations or even from the wit and repartee of urban sophisticates and their glamorous scrapes. Rather it's comedy that derives from the texture of everyday life; from banter with an old friend, from trying to get to work on time or impressing a girl, from social misunderstandings, from our own failings that keep dragging us down.

1 'What Happened to You, Whatever Happened to Me?' The Story of *The Likely Lads*

The first episode of *The Likely Lads* aired on BBC 2 on the evening of 16 December 1964. It began at 9.55pm, just after Ed Wynn introduced 'top-line' variety from the USA and before a short news bulletin, leading to a cello recital. The show's journey to the screen was a classic case of being in the right place at the right time. Dick Clement, who worked for the BBC in radio, was taking a television production course and was asked to make a short film. He used a script he had written for the BBC's amateur dramatic troupe, the Ariel Players, with a Geordie friend he had met a couple of years earlier in a pub in Notting Hill, Ian La Frenais.[1] The scene they penned featured two male friends talking about two women they see in a café and the women in turn commenting on their new admirers – it was the basis for the second episode in the first series, 'Double Date'.

According to BBC Memos in May 1964, on the basis of this sketch the BBC's Head of Comedy, Duncan Wood, the man who produced *Hancock* (BBC 1957–61) and *Steptoe and Son* (BBC 1962–5, 70–4), commissioned three scripts with the option of three more. In July, on seeing these scripts he decided that 'on the quality of the writing so far … we should take up the option forthwith'.[2] According to Dick Clement, the sketch was championed by Marty Feldman (later a familiar face in absurdist TV comedy shows like *At Last the 1948 Show,* Associated Rediffusion 1967) and legendary producer Dennis Main Wilson.

> BBC 2 was just starting up – I was hauled back from the Norfolk Broads on holiday into Michael Peacock's office [the first controller of the BBC 2 channel], and he said, 'Do you see this as a six-part series?'. What are you going to say? 'Absolutely.' We said yes and suddenly Ian and I were professional writers.[3]

Thus BBC 2's first sitcom began. If this birth story sounds vaguely familiar, it is – nearly forty years later *The Office* (2001–3) started in very similar circumstances, with a sketch for Stephen Merchant's BBC production course.

Rising young stars James Bolam and Rodney Bewes were cast as Terry and Bob. After the death of the appointed director, Harry Carlisle, Wood installed Clement as producer and director, a daunting task for a young man who had not previously worked in TV, but one he seems to have performed manfully. The files on the show at the BBC's Written Archives Centre at Caversham are full of tactful and polite memos from Clement to all levels of crew involved in production and to numerous organisations that supplied locations and props. He describes the process as follows:

> I was very green ... to be doing five-camera situation comedy with a studio audience, which is a very specialised technique, was quite something ... in those days you couldn't easily do retakes, you did it in three days and if anything went wrong you'd go back to the beginning.[4]

Clement is hugely positive about his experience at the BBC, especially the crews and support he received and the three-week directing course that spawned the show. 'They gave you the best people to talk to and ask how to do it ... I have nothing but happy memories of [the BBC at that time].'[5]

I discovered the only note of institutional discord in the archives and, although Clement has no memory of it, it offers an interesting vignette on the cultural tensions of the time. Keen to get viewers to the show, Clement wrote to say that he was concerned with the lack of promotion in the *Radio Times* and some errors in the publicity material. From the Caversham files we can see that he received replies of astonishing peevishness from the powers that be. To his point that there had been little emphasis on the two stars (they are described as 'two young Northern actors', making them sound like unknowns despite extensive film and theatre credits), the TV editor of *Radio Times* argued that 'the fact is that neither Bewes or Bolam is well known'[6] and the head of publicity airily claimed to have asked around the office and that no one had heard of them, rather misunderstanding the idea of publicity.

The press release for the first series does offer an interesting insight, however. Its main aim is to explain the show's title to an uncomprehending Fleet Street and set some kind of context for the comedy. It also aims to position the show as part of a 60s' zeitgeist, as if to say, 'The BBC stuffy and elitist? No! Look at this! Northern and on BBC 2!'. Entitled 'Meet the Likely Lads', it begins: 'In the North the old men in factories chew their plug tobacco and shake their heads watching the younger lads, the apprentices, and they might say of some of them – "there's a likely 'un".' It goes on to suggest that Bob and Terry are just such lads, but also that they are two among many; 'hundreds of lads like Bob Ferris and Terry Collier. ... acquisitive, irreverent, they don't miss much. At their age, naturally, they're idealists – but injected with a strong shot of Northern common sense.' An earlier draft couched the prevailing philosophy rather differently. It ended with 'Everything's happening now and most of it's good, the future's something that comes along after you're twenty-five.'[7] As we shall see, this is somewhat ironic – Clement and La Frenais' scripts are imbued with melancholy about the past and worries about the future.

As producer, Clement had to keep a tight rein on all aspects of the frugal budget, in fact underspending on the first series by £2,467. The show stayed relatively low budget throughout, rising from just under £2,000 per episode in the first series to just over £6,000 by the third. Costs varied according to the scripts – the series, like most TV fiction of the time, was very much a studio production – but a few episodes like the first, 'Entente Cordiale', had small scenes requiring film inserts and locations.[8]

In one crucial aspect the BBC failed the programme, although this was not immediately evident. In the early 60s recording technology for video was not long established. Equipment and tape costs were extraordinarily high, resulting in pressure within the corporation to save money by reusing tapes. Most of the first series survived but once established the programme became fair game for the accountants and cost-efficiency experts. After their repeat run, all the second series and all but two of the third series were recycled as game shows and regional news bulletins.

This policy has long been rightly condemned, but the BBC was subject to cultural as well as economic pressures. Television was thought to be an ephemeral, disposable medium that could not aspire to art unless it replicated existing high culture. Once a programme, especially an entertainment show, was shown and repeated, its life was thought to be at an end. The powers that be lacked the imagination to envisage the possibility of developing home recording and failed to see how their own product could resonate with future audiences.

Public appeals, such as the BFI's 'Missing, Believed Wiped' initiative and the BBC's 'Treasure Hunt', have filled a few significant gaps in our television heritage. Sometimes fans recorded the screen with 8mm or 16mm cameras and occasionally a few tapes were retrieved from skips by concerned crew. In the case of *The Likely Lads*, the opener 'Entente Cordiale' and one episode from Series 2, 'The Last of the Big Spenders', have reappeared (the latter ruefully dismissed by an embarrassed Clement and La Frenais as a 'potboiler – and we knew it at the time'[9]). There are also rumours on the collectors' circuit of two more, 'A Star is Born' and 'Far-away Places', existing in private hands.

Fortunately, the BBC was more careful with their paperwork; all the scripts from the series exist, and I was able to read these at the BBC Written Archives Centre at Caversham. Twelve out of twenty

episodes made in the 60s' series are probably gone for good as
television, but at least the words survive. I have analysed some of these
episodes in the book on the basis of the scripts because they add to our
understanding of the series. Some of them are up there with the very best
moments in British sitcom, let alone the show itself; 'Where Have all the
Flowers Gone?', the last episode of the second series, and 'Friends and
Neighbours' and 'Love and Marriage' from the third series are
particularly fine and their absence is a loss to TV heritage.

    The Likely Lads was screened on a minority channel, one,
furthermore, that initially was only available to viewers in London and
the Midlands (ironically not the North East). How then did it become a
popular and enduring success? The answer lies in the much-derided
British TV ritual of repeats. Mainstream audiences across the country
first became aware of the lads just a couple of weeks after the show
began to air, when a specially written sketch featuring Bob and Terry's
encyclopaedic knowledge of Rupert Bear annuals was shown on BBC 1's
holiday extravaganza *Christmas Night with the Stars*. Clement explains
that 'It got a big response so they repeated [the series] on BBC 1 ... it
suddenly pushed it into some kind of orbit.'[10] There were three series
with an initial run on BBC 2, now gradually spreading across Britain,
followed just a few months later by a repeat of the whole series on
BBC 1.[11] Also, whereas the BBC 2 screening was at around 9.55pm, the
BBC 1 repeats were much earlier in primetime, at 7.30pm, so before
the exodus to numerous provincial Roxy ballrooms or Wheatsheafs for
the target demographic of young working-class people. Repeats have
proved vital to sitcoms over the years, pulling in new audiences directed
to the series through word of mouth, and allowing the opportunity for
viewers to deepen their relationship with the characters on screen.

    We can see how viewers responded to the show through
audience research reports, produced for internal use by the BBC. These
used a 'reaction index' of up to 100, with detailed responses from a
cross-section of the audience. The numbers on this index are
consistently high: 69 for the first episode, 'Entente Cordiale', and 76 for
the second, 'Double Date'. The comments are a fascinating insight into

the realities of public opinion at the time; aside from the occasional worry about crudity when children could be watching, and an 'utterly disgusting' from one Doctor Martin, 'the great majority of reporting viewers seem in fact to have liked it very much'.[12] Views included 'a good working-class story without the kitchen sink', 'portrayed exactly the true feeling of class distinction in a Northern factory', 'difficult to imagine that we are not eavesdropping on the lives of a real couple of friends', 'so realistic of young viewers' lives consisting of birds, pubs and fun' and 'an excellent tonic for the end of a tiring day'. Significantly, working-class viewers were particularly favourable to the show, seeing it as authentic without being worthy and patronising. One comment from a presumably aspirant secretary that it is 'common' only serves to underline this.[13]

The 60s' series of *The Likely Lads*, while taking an ambiguous attitude to the future, present and past, does have a sheen of modernity that marked it out from some other elements of the schedule and other sitcoms. Its youthful heroes and their attitudes were part of this, but so was the presentation and *mise en scène*. The first series has a jaunty title sequence with an upbeat jazzy score and stills of the lads at play taken at artful angles. Indeed, the montage of stills, reminiscent of films of the time, is used as a device quite often to move the narrative along, for instance in 'Double Date' and 'Goodbye to All That'.

This was all a very deliberate strategy by Clement and La Frenais. Their influences were far away from the comic mainstream in Britain at the time; indeed, in many respects they were not comic at all. La Frenais has said that '*The Likely Lads* as a series owes its conception more to drama.'[14] Both writers are clear that their principal televisual influence was in fact Troy Kennedy Martin's police series *Z Cars* (BBC 1963–78); Clement says, 'I'm always at pains to point up *Z Cars* as one of our great influences ... the cops were real people and the problems they were talking about were real.'[15] La Frenais argues, 'Before Hancock, comedy was set in drawing rooms, which really had no interest to either of us. The big changing point was *Z Cars*, which was a drama series but was about the reality.' What he and Clement wanted to do was to take 'this kind of realism, but find a comedic way into this world'.[16] Their primary influence, though, was cinema and it is important to note that, despite their command and respect for television as a medium, Clement and La Frenais have always seen films as a career goal.[17]

In particular, *The Likely Lads* is defined by the British New Wave films that just preceded it. Between *Room at the Top* (d. Jack Clayton 1959) and *This Sporting Life* (d. Lindsay Anderson 1963), a handful of titles revolutionised the conception of what British moving image culture could be. Suddenly the national screen was not dominated by the likes of Kenneth More and his crinkly hair or 'decent chaps doing their bit', but allowed a raw irreverence and, crucially, the representation of ordinary working-class people, especially from the industrial North.

Often formally relegated to comic chars or bellyaching privates, working-class characters (and the actors who played them) were now centre stage. Subsequent critical opinion has been harsh on the British New Wave[18] and there is a sense of Hampstead 'discovering' the North in some of them, but moments transcend any such critique. When Albert Finney snarls 'Whatever you say I am, that's what I'm Not' in *Saturday Night and Sunday Morning* (d. Karel Reisz 1960), or Tom Courteney stops just before the finishing line in the climactic race of *The Loneliness of the Long Distance Runner* (d. Tony Richardson 1962), sneering at the borstal governor who tried to patronise him, or indeed when fear stops Courtenay as *Billy Liar* (d. John Schlesinger 1963) from boarding that train to London, there is a palpable kick of the real, an emotional energy aiming to communicate directly with the viewer.

The Likely Lads offers a comic angle on the New Wave's concerns, although it is a reworking of the scenarios with wittier dialogue and funnier situations rather than a parody. The series was cast so that audiences would make the connection with the films.[19] James Bolam had a small role in *A Kind of Loving* (d. John Schlesinger 1962) and played Tom Courteney's best friend in *The Loneliness of the Long Distance Runner*. Rodney Bewes played Billy's friend Arthur in *Billy*

13

Liar. Clement and La Frenais wanted to draw on this New Wave pedigree to make the audience feel they were encountering something authentic and of the time. While the tone is lighter (although I would argue the resonance is often deeper), there are a number of parallels that can be drawn between the series and these films. There is the fear of settling down and of domesticity (featured in *A Kind of Loving*'s terror of being trapped and tied down by marriage); there are Bob's dreams of aspiration, reminiscent again of Vic Brown's ambition in the same film and Joe Lampton's rise in *Room at the Top*; Terry has the whiff of an uncontrollable rebel in the vein of Arthur Seaton in *Saturday Night and Sunday Morning*; and most of all there are the failed dreams and lack of confidence of *Billy Liar*.[20] The background to the lads' adventures is very familiar from the New Wave – chasing girls, drudgery and camaraderie at work, nights at the pub – but also the pressures to settle down and the dreams of leaving (symbolised in the films by the trains that never get taken, the inability to find the courage to really go). In 'The Talk of the Town' the show even tackles that staple of social realist kitchen sink drama, the unwanted pregnancy, for comic effect. Bob drunkenly announces an engagement with a girlfriend, Helen, and then becomes convinced she must be pregnant by her attempts to contact him. She is – but it's not his, she just wanted to tell him she was already engaged to Duggie, newly returned from sea.

Instead of creating drama or direct political comment from the everyday grind, the 60s' show uses it as a source of comedy. Despite its earthiness, this humour is sophisticated and subtle, exploring the absurdities and joys of being young working-class men, and nudging viewers to relate them to their lives. Those more familiar with *Whatever Happened to the Likely Lads?* will find the characters of Bob and Terry are there already, complete with the attitudes that define them. While their social status is roughly equal it is clearly established that Bob wants more, that he is hungry for betterment and more economic security. Terry is equally determined to live for the present and just wants to get by, often by the skin of his teeth, as he fibs, skives and sponges.

The 60s' series ended on 23 July 1966, just as England progressed through the quarter-finals of their triumphant World Cup campaign. In a particularly deft finishing touch 'Goodbye to All That' sees Bob sign up for the Army Electrical Corps only to find himself discharged for flat feet, just as Terry signs on to be with his best mate. The series thus came to an apparently natural end. Why then did it come back to our screens six and a half years later (a gap that becomes five in the world of the show)?

Clement and La Frenais describe it as the result of 'curious telepathy', both thinking of the possibility at the same time. They found that people had kept asking the question 'Whatever happened to those two?'. La Frenais has said that 'so many changes had happened to Britain' that they wanted to explore those through the characters and 'ideas just poured on to the page'.[21] Meanwhile, Clement told me, 'We thought of them before we thought of Britain … the changes that happen to you between twenty and twenty-five are huge … it seemed such a rich field, and then you added to that the changes in society.'[22]

So the boys returned – reunited by chance on the Edinburgh express in a power cut in 'Strangers on a Train'. This was a neat move as the circumstances forced them to confront the parting of years earlier and patch up their quarrel. This reunion naturally led to both laughs and pathos, they were now abutting thirty and their golden youth was behind them. The certainties of the community they grew up in were vanishing fast too. A crucial element was the introduction of Thelma as Bob's fiancée, a new point of comic conflict between the lads. Brigit Forsyth, as Thelma, became an important third presence and another point of possible identification for viewers in the series.

There were a number of structural and production changes that came at the same time as this new leading character. This time Clement relieved himself of production duties, taken over by James Gilbert and then Bernard Thompson.[23] Although much of the show is based in the interior of pubs and in rooms, there is considerably more film and location shooting than in the 60s. While, in the BBC tradition, there were some shots of West London streets handily round the corner

15

from TV Centre, this time they did venture North – something that never happened the first time round. This can be seen not only in the sweeping shots of Tyneside wastelands that inform some of the ideas of loss and social change, but also in the key scenes based around Bob's new house on the Elm Lodge housing estate. This is actually a real house, in Agincourt on the then newly built Hillfields estate in Killingworth, just a couple of miles north east of Newcastle city centre. A family, the Whalens, lived there and vacated the house for shooting, and crews spent much time on the estate.[24] It's still there and largely unchanged – surely it's time to add a blue plaque.

The scripts were organised differently too. Whereas in the 60s each episode was largely self-contained, this time there were storylines running across episode and a large degree of continuity from one to the next. In all there were just two series, although of unusually long runs of thirteen episodes each. The first ran from 9 January to 3 April 1973,

16

Bob's house – today

culminating in Bob's wedding, and the second in a similar slot in 1974.[25] Broadcast was now on BBC 1, thus seeking, and capturing, a mass audience from the start.

The response to the show was positive both critically and commercially from the start. Ratings were high, with around 25 per cent of the population watching. Appreciation indexes were again very favourable, especially for the first series. Responses from the newspaper reviewers, then important arbiters of television taste, were positively ecstatic across the tabloids and the broadsheets alike. *The Sun* said, 'Whatever happened to the Likely Lads? They got funnier, that's what'; Peter Black in the *Daily Mail* argued that the show 'was BBC character comedy at its unbeaten best', while Sean Day-Lewis in the *Daily Telegraph* called it 'the most effective situation comedy produced on television in the present decade' and Nancy Banks-Smith, then as now of *The Guardian*, pronounced it 'funny and true … funny is truth and truth is funny and that is all script writers need to know'.[26]

After the second series, the lads returned one more time to the small screen in a Christmas Eve special in 1974, one of the funniest episodes of all. And then it was all over – at least on TV. In 1973, as Clement and La Frenais wrote that final series, Duncan Wood, still in the BBC corridors of comedy power, sent a memo saying, 'it seems probable that after these shows the *Likely Lads* writing vein will be exhausted',[27] and sought to contract Clement and La Frenais to new projects. The result of this was, eventually, *Porridge* (BBC 1973–7), their other timeless classic.

It was not all quite over, however. In the 1970s, the British film industry was on its knees as television triumphed. One of the very few ways to bring in audiences was to make film versions of their favourite TV shows; usually sitcoms as they were less bound by plot and had a wide audience base. Though these films proved commercially popular (famously, the first film based on *On the Buses* was the biggest British hit of 1971, beating James Bond), they were rarely artistic successes. The longer running time and a more expansive medium saw most spin-offs trying to broaden their appeal by taking characters out of their regular

17

situation, typically on holiday, or expanding situations from old episodes. This rarely works – the original economy and charm are lost and there is not sufficient attention given to the different kind of spectatorship in cinema.

It is telling that Clement and La Frenais, with their cinematic aspirations, made the two most compelling films from sitcoms. The film version of *Porridge* (d. Clement 1979) is consistently interesting and introduces a plot line that can be sustained for ninety minutes. The film of *The Likely Lads* (d. Michael Tuchner), made a year or so after the series ended and released in 1976, is also largely successful. While it does introduce the inevitable holiday sequence (a caravanning trip to Northumberland that does at least include one of the best jokes in British cinema – while playing bridge very badly Terry goes outside to relieve himself very loudly against the side of the caravan. His embarrassed girlfriend apologises, only for Thelma, his exasperated bridge partner, to say 'Don't worry, it's the first time I've known what's in his hand all night'), the first part of the film and its conclusion expand on the themes of the series. Bob suffers a mid-life crisis and is forced to think through his fears of the future and his struggle for conformity; Terry, meanwhile, flirts with domesticity and is also rehoused to a new, and already decaying, tower block.

Clement and La Frenais both have their reservations about the film. Clement recounts that they had to remain in the USA during filming, so were unable to go on set, although there were extensive rewrites on the insistence of James Bolam, while La Frenais grudgingly acknowledged that 'there's a couple of things that are corny but it's not embarrassing'.[28] Yet, for all its occasionally episodic and disjointed nature, the film adds to our understanding of the series and forms a fitting end to our acquaintance with the lads. The film had been planned even before *Whatever Happened to the Likely Lads?* and did well at the box office for its makers EMI, although the BBC coined much of the revenue as part of the deal.[29]

To understand *The Likely Lads* we need to understand the talents that created the programme. Since that precipitous meeting at the

Uxbridge Arms, London W11, Dick Clement and Ian La Frenais have worked together almost exclusively ever since, although Clement's producing and directing work has sometimes led to solo writing assignments for La Frenais on shows like *Spender* (BBC 1991–3).

Dick Clement was born in Southend-on-Sea and is middle class, quintessentially English and long a family man. Ian La Frenais is a Geordie, from Whitley Bay, a seaside town near the mouth of the Tyne. He too had a comfortable background though, the son of a corporate accountant, and attended public school.[30] He married much later in life and has maintained a more laddish image, particularly in his adherence to football and rock'n'roll – Tracey Ullman has dubbed him 'the ultimate rock groupie'.[31]

Both were only in their mid-twenties when their big break came with the commission for *The Likely Lads*, Clement already on the BBC staff as a production assistant and La Frenais working in market research. The show quickly established their reputation as scriptwriters, and also their distinctive style, based, as La Frenais claims, on 'natural speech' and 'believability – it does come out of characters'.[32]

In the mid-70s they both moved to Hollywood, where they have spent most of their time ever since. This move followed the success of *Porridge*, when an American producer invited them to make an American version, *On the Rocks* (ABC 1975–6). This was only moderately successful, but, whatever their frustrations with the US networks, Hollywood also offered a way in to the film world that had always fascinated them. They had been involved in British film productions (such as *Otley*, d. Clement 1968) in the gap between the *Likely Lads* series but it was clear that the remnants of the British film industry would not support their aspirations.

The lifestyle in LA is obviously attractive and over the past three decades they have really had two parallel careers. On the one hand, they have written for films; sometimes as credited writers on projects that bear their stamp, *The Commitments* (d. Alan Parker 1991) and *Still Crazy* (d. Brian Gibson 1998), for example. Much of their Hollywood work, however, has been as 'script doctors', a lucrative but

19

uncredited tinsel town task, improving work that lacks a certain verve. In Clement and La Frenais' case, this has tended, unsurprisingly, to be polishing dialogue, typically in otherwise less-than-erudite action films like *The Rock* and *Bad Boys 2* (both d. Michael Bay 1996, 2000).

On the other hand, alongside this work they have not abandoned either television or Britain. They have produced numerous works for British television and have stayed connected to British life; 'I like our names still being around here,' says La Frenais.[33] This work has included more sitcoms, not all of which have proved as resilient as *The Likely Lads*, and adaptations like *The Rotters' Club* (BBC 2005), from the novel on life in the 70s by Jonathan Coe. Since *Porridge* their main contribution has been to develop a whole new genre, one that has gained increasing importance within the medium in recent years; comedy-drama. They did this primarily through their third great TV work, *Auf Wiedersehen Pet* (Witzend/Central/ITV 1983–6). This told the story of a group of English builders (a Cockney, a Brummie, a Bristolian, a Scouser and, inevitably, several Geordies) working in Germany, and later all over the world. Its tone was certainly traceable to *The Likely Lads*, but it was less dependent on laughs and built up the turmoil of its characters and their era. Structurally, too, episodes were longer and there was no studio audience, 'I began to hate the studio audience,' La Frenais claims,[34] predating the big aesthetic and structural changes in British TV comedy by some years. The BBC revived the series successfully for two series and a special (2001–4), informing the comedy-drama genre it had helped to create.

What *Auf Wiedersehen Pet*, and indeed their other work to a degree, shows is the strengths that were evident early on in *The Likely Lads*. There is empathy, a warmth in dealing with the characters they create, a curiosity in exploring aspects of everyday life and how it affects the soul – and of course a feel for dialogue, for the ebb and flow of conversation, particularly between men who don't have power or real ownership over their own lives. In that respect, there is a direct line from Bob and Terry to Fletch and Godber in *Porridge* to Nev and Oz in *Auf Wiedersehen Pet*.

20

Despite its popularity and status, for some years *The Likely Lads* threatened to become just a fond folk memory. The 60s' show has only survived as a fragment rather than in full, and the 70s' show, after acclaim and success throughout that decade, went a long time without being screened before all the surviving programmes were shown again in the mid-1990s. Now that they are all on DVD they can live and breathe again with new audiences – away from the broadcast flow they originally inhabited, they still stand up as some of the finest writing that British TV culture, never mind just sitcom, has produced.

Naturally, there is more to the series than the product of a creative partnership of two individuals, as fruitful as that is. It is also the product of an institution, the BBC, and a medium, popular television. At the time it was broadcast there was a system in place in which creative talent could be indulged and developed and, as a result, the very best work could reach the public.

In the 60s and 70s, TV was unequivocally the dominant mass entertainment medium in Britain, run through a duopoly between BBC and ITV that had its own equilibrium, producing a creative tension that just seemed to work. The duopoly undoubtedly had many faults – it was a closed market, it could encourage complacency and so on – but many of its effects proved benign. After the Pilkington Report of 1962 hammered ITV for its commercialism, the BBC received new powers and resources. Assured of its position, it also began to understand popular tastes, becoming engaging rather than elitist. It has been said that the duopoly that resulted post-Pilkington made the BBC work to be more popular and ITV strive for more quality.[35] Certainly, the BBC knew it had to connect with all licence-payers, including those beyond its traditional middle-class base. *The Likely Lads* is a direct result of the quest for young, working-class audiences.

The duopoly, because it created a status quo in which the BBC and ITV did not threaten each other's existence, allowed talent to be nurtured and risks to be taken. The BBC could take a chance on a young production assistant and his mate from down the pub and give them the freedom to produce what they wanted to make. It was also helped by the

21

attitude of the people at the top in the 60s, notably the director-general Hugh Greene, and the second head of BBC 2, David Attenborough, who took over from Peacock in 1965, and has long retained the status of agreed national treasure. As Andrew Crisell says, 'Greene commanded the loyalty of his staff by being relaxed and liberal, affording freedom and flexibility to programme makers and performers.'[36] With him, Attenborough and executive producers like Duncan Wood, creative talents knew they would be supported, and that they would be able to respond to what was happening around them, as dramas like *Cathy Come Home* (BBC 1966) did with social iniquities. Programmes on the BBC (and indeed ITV) could reflect changing times and, like many episodes of *The Likely Lads*, talk about life as it is lived. The show was able to be quite risqué in its treatment of sex and pushed boundaries in showing Bob and Terry's laddish behaviour. Reaction to this was broadly positive from the public and allowed writers to continue to explore reality.

By the time of *Whatever Happened to the Likely Lads?* the television industry had matured, and so had its audience. They understood what the medium could do and it was now long established as one of the premier forms of artistic communication in British society. Proven talents like Clement and La Frenais were free to create complex characters and worlds; guaranteed large audiences by the limits of the marketplace, programmes could make viewers work to divine meanings from what they were seeing. In a multichannel world that becomes harder – it is easy for us as an audience to make the least demanding choice. Subsumed by the immediate and the instant, it is harder to find material that really resonates, that tells us something we don't already know but want to hear.

However, it is not impossible today to produce programmes, like *The Likely Lads*, that interrogate their own audience. Comedy can still do this, as Gervais and Merchant demonstrated with *The Office*. For all the years of talk of the decline of the sitcom, it is a durable form that, when it finds an audience, can deliver enough to keep market, hearts and brains happy.

Whatever Happened to the Likely Lads? is one of a number of sitcoms from the 70s that still work thirty years on. As well as Bob and Terry, characters like Fletch, Reginald Perrin, Miss Jones, Captain Mainwaring, Basil Fawlty and Margo Leadbetter still resonate. This period established sitcom as one of our richest artistic forms, one that suited a mode of British expression. The shows produced then have created reference points recognised by people far too young to have seen them when first broadcast. This has occurred through extensive repeats but also because they have entered the national consciousness as a body of work that reflects a national self-image, and one from which we can unearth truths about ourselves.

2 'Tomorrow's Almost Over': The Life and Times of *The Likely Lads*

We feel so immersed in the world of the lads because we are immersed in their times. To the audience that saw the shows when they were originally broadcast this was the time they were living in – to those of us who have viewed them in retrospect they shine a light on our recent history and help us to understand the way we are now. While dating very little, Clement and La Frenais' writing is extraordinarily sensitive and reflexive about the historical moment, and how it can impact on ordinary people.

This is not unique. Much of the best TV writing of the 60s and 70s was explicitly trying to tackle the problems of the age, from *Z Cars* to the social problems examined and explored in single-play slots like *The Wednesday Play* (BBC 1964–70) and *Play for Today* (BBC 1970–84). Comedy was also part of this. Many shows of this time create laughs from points of social conflict and characters discuss what is happening in the wider world. The audience understood and expected this, seeing no contradiction in combining entertainment and social comment. The two top-rated sitcoms of the 1960s, *Till Death Us Do Part* (by Johnny Speight, BBC 1966–75) and *Steptoe and Son* (by Ray Galton and Alan Simpson), made their reputations partly on this collision of laughter and social analysis. In the former, ageing reactionary Alf Garnett pontificated from his Wapping living room on his fears of change and argued with his left-wing son-in-law on the country's direction. In *Steptoe* the conflicts were less stark, but frequently Galton and Simpson made Albert and Harold stand for different social attitudes to add fuel to the fire of their comic conflict. This was a public discussion, a way of society coming to terms with the questions that it faced and working towards some kind of answers. Television was a forum through which this could happen and comic characters acted as a kind of proxy for viewers, allowing them to think through the questions that were raised at one remove. It has to be remembered, for those of you reared on timeshifting, downloads and DVD box sets, that television was both a truly mass medium and a collective activity in the 60s and 70s.

The Likely Lads offers an unusually explicit conversation between text and audience. This is for a number of reasons. First, the lads themselves are so 'normal'. Most people would at least like to think that the Steptoes' situation was extreme and unusual, and consider Alf to be something of an exaggeration (even if they are unfortunately mistaken). Bob and Terry lead 'typical' lives, not rich, but, unlike the Steptoes', not too poor, too unlucky, to seem part of shared or understood experience. Second, they are young so have the time and inclination, and sometimes the money, to be able to be part of the modern society; to go out and have fun, to take their place in the consumer revolution. They also talk about their situation a lot, what's happening around them, what might be waiting for them in the wider world. Lastly, the gap between the two shows – the years that separate the broadcast of *The Likely Lads* and *Whatever Happened to the Likely Lads?* – draws attention to social change.

There was a big gap in *Steptoe* too but little had altered; indeed the point was that little had altered, adding another layer of desperation to Harold's miserable existence. By contrast, when Terry returns from the Army he finds that everything has changed. His friends are domesticated, including his best friend who has also entered a different

25

'The Go-Go? Gone?'

social sphere from the one they inhabited together previously. More than that, all the places he knew have gone. In 'Moving On' Bob drives him round their youthful haunts, now a mass of ruined brickwork, building sites and new developments. At the top of a multi-storey car park he tells him that they are standing on the site of the Go-Go rock club, eliciting the plaintive response, 'The Go-Go? Gone?'. The culmination of this is the discovery that the new civic centre has been built over the Roxy, the site of their former glories as North Tyneside's young blades, boozers and lotharios. All that seems left is Eric's fish and chip shop, the only building still standing in miles of rubble-strewn wasteland. 'None of our memories is intact,' Terry wails.

In doing this the series is tapping into a wider mindset, as change, both in modes of thinking and in the visible march of modernity transforming the landscape, was affecting much of what everyone did, saw and understood. It is natural for Terry to comment on this change, and be fearful of its effects on him, and likewise for Bob and Thelma, who are benefiting in many ways from it, to make the case for its advantage. As Ian La Frenais suggests, 'Terry was coming back as a displaced person, they had bypassed him, these changes – which was great for us because Bob had embraced them and was influenced by everything that was changing socially.'[37]

Of course Bob and Terry are not real people, but they are constructed realistically. Clement and La Frenais give them a history, an identifiable background and a place in a specific location and timeframe. In this light change would have been a constant in the lads' lives, certainly in contrast to earlier generations of the imagined Ferris and Collier families. As written and understood by the audience, they would have been brought up in an impoverished but settled environment based on family, neighbourhood and, for the men at least, work – in their case probably in the shipyards. This worldview is described in Richard Hoggart's classic study of working-class culture, *The Uses of Literacy*, published in 1957, as 'the personal, the concrete, the local'.[38] There was the Depression in the 30s, but the structure of communities and culture had survived. Bob and Terry are created as war babies, born at the height of the blitz (a start in life that acts as a prologue to the feature-film version). They would be toddlers in the austerity years, but benefit (if that is the right word, given their memories of the experience) from greater education provision, and certainly a welfare system that meant they didn't go hungry and were unlikely to die in infancy.

For many of their generation, rock'n'roll and the teenage revolution took a hold and, for the first time, they were part of a global rather than a local culture. TV itself became an important mode of communication, bringing the outside world to the home and opening up vistas beyond the Tyne. Most importantly they are shown as the first generation of Ferrises and Colliers to make a reasonable sum of money and have things to spend it on beyond rent, food and beer. When we join the lads at twenty-one they have jobs and inhabit a world where wages are much higher, relatively and actually, than their fathers would ever have earned, and this disposable income for the masses creates a leisure

27

economy enabling them to spend it. New places to go, new things to eat and new things to do are all available now for the common man. In the 60s' show Bob and Terry get to go abroad on holiday, visit steakhouses, casinos and cocktail bars for the first time, as well as maintaining their cultural heritage at The Black Horse and at Newcastle United home matches. Their mothers and sisters are also able to step away from domestic servitude, at least in practical terms through affordable labour-saving devices in the home, and might begin to question the imbalance of opportunity between the sexes, even if they met stiff resistance from their menfolk.[39]

From 1964–6, the original run, England was, after all, supposed to be 'swinging'. In the provincial life most people led it wasn't all boutiques and champagne, but people were becoming aware that there were other ways of doing things, the possibility that more choices might be open to them, even if it was far from true that the old restrictions, expectations and hierarchies had been cast off. Now at least there was the potential, however illusory the actuality, that the limits placed on their lives could be overcome. This debate was happening in culture at large as well, and was a matter of political and popular debate.

In the North this confidence had been manifested in the previous few years with the New Wave films and even the rise of The Beatles. The industrial Northern working class was, for one thing, a very large chunk of the population. Now Britain was ostensibly booming through its industrial power – the industrial working class and their communities could demand a voice and a share in the wealth they created. As average weekly earnings rose by 130 per cent between 1955 and 1969, they became an eagerly sought after commercial constituency.[40]

A few years on in the early 70s and the picture was much more complicated. On the one hand, some of the ideas questioning the social apparatus that in the 60s were the preserve of a vanguard of intellectuals or students were now part of mainstream discourse. The women's movement, sexual liberation, radical action by disadvantaged minority groups and the questioning of some of the old tenets of the British way of life, including working-class life, like marriage or work were suddenly open to debate. Even Terry declares that 'marriage is an outdated institution' and that 'I have dropped out of the rat race'. On the other hand, there is a backlash to these new freedoms by those summarised gloomily by Terry in the first episode as 'Malcolm Muggeridge, Lord Longford and the Jesus revolution', keen to make sure that the bohemian ideas once safely confined to the privileged few did not drip down to the hoi polloi. This was coupled with a severe economic downturn, brewing for years, but which became obvious to most after the devaluation of the pound in 1967, the year after the first incarnation of Bob and Terry left our screens.[41]

Suddenly, there were dark clouds on the horizon of all this new-found prosperity, and a fear that it might all be taken away again. Understandably, once ordinary folk had had a TV set, a fridge, the chance to take holidays on sunny foreign beaches and something to show for all their grind and toil, they were unwilling to return to austerity. The year when the first series of *Whatever Happened to the Likely Lads?* was filmed, 1972, saw the highest number of strike days in British history as workers resisted wage restraint and job cuts.[42] As the second series screened at the start of 1974, the energy crisis meant a national three-day week and nights in the dark, gathering miserably round a candle as the TV and light bulbs suddenly shut up shop without warning.[43] I remember, as an eight-year-old, finding this thoroughly disconcerting; to people brought up in the deprivations of the 30s and 40s it must have been profoundly depressing, a shift back to those dark ages of frequent cold, hunger and struggle.

Anxiety, then, was a key emotion for many in the early 70s, a knot in the stomach worrying that the money you earned might be worth nothing as inflation inched over 10 per cent and interest rates soared, that the possessions you had acquired might be taken from you and that your children might not have as good a life as you did. The deprivation and austerity of the recent past remained at the back of the mind as a fearful memory for the newly affluent.

A collective mindset has since taken on the 60s and 70s with gusto. The 60s are a sort of national obsession for the British in the media and popular discourse, but one touched with ambivalence. In one sense, it is looked back on as the last great national victory, the last time the rest of the world really cared about what we said or did. The 1966 World Cup is the new Trafalgar, The Beatles and other denizens of the swinging decade the equivalent of the imperial generals that decorate Westminster squares, as new generations discover the iconography of the period. There is a considerable amount of reinvention; one would think now that everyone had flowers in their hair as well as pounds in their pocket. The tensions of the time live on in some ways, in the frequent accusations that the supposed hedonism, free expression and easy cash of the 60s weakened our moral fibre. Certain criminal cases of the decade are obsessively recalled, particularly the Moors murders, still providing front pages forty years on, but also the Kray Twins, the Great Train Robbers and the Mary Bell case.[44] It's as if this is a price we are made to pay for all that pleasure; the worm of decay that came in the golden apple of a TV in every home and double overtime. Even just a few years after they finished, the 60s were being looked back on nostalgically, not least by Bob and Terry. 'Great days, Terry,' Bob enthuses, as he recalls their mid-60s heyday at the Roxy ballroom. Already the era has acquired a rosy glow, partly, as we will see, because of their own history, but also because Bob recognises a collective pride in being part of the era.

In contrast, for about fifteen years after New Year's Eve 1979, the 70s were treated as a national guilty secret, gently swept under the carpet whenever raised. There were exceptional, although contested moments; for some the rise of punk rock, for quite another group the rise of Margaret Thatcher, might be celebrated. However, as well as being at the end of the decade these were also movements that in their different ways reacted violently against the prevailing trends of the time, that despised the despondency and defeatism that seemed to characterise the period.

Now the view has changed. Somewhere in the 90s the 70s became cosy and kitsch. A reinvented 70s now exists, all platform boots and themed nightclubs with comedy wigs.[45] This historical airbrushing has only recently started to be challenged. For the 70s, despite, or maybe because of, all the anxiety felt by those living through it, is a fascinating time. It was television, including sitcoms, that measured the temperature of the times, raising the anxieties, contradictions and challenges of the 70s for the audience, without easy answers or solutions being provided.

In the last two or three years, the Britain of the twenty-first century has woken up to the fascination and the complexity of the 70s, seeing beyond the idea of it as a repository of strikes, bombs, uncollected rubbish and early closing, while also rejecting the rebranding as party central, replete with wacky costumes and spacehoppers. This might be partly due to those born in the 70s coming to the age where they are curious about the world they entered, or it might be boredom with the platitudes and depoliticisation of the Blair era, so that battles of ideas and opposing ways of seeing the world become attractive again.

The phenomenal success of the BBC series *Life on Mars* (Kudos/BBC 2006–7) is an interesting indication of this new approach to the period. In this programme, modern Manchester detective Sam Tyler is somehow transported in time to the city in 1973 (during transmission of the first series of *Whatever Happened to the Likely Lads?*). In its attitude to the period *Life on Mars* has its cake and gorges on it. While the device of Sam Tyler presents a progressive modern approach to issues like race, sexuality and women, much of the popularity of the show derived from the modern audience revelling in the 'politically incorrect' retorts of 70s' cop DCI Gene Hunt to Tyler's progressive stances, and in the show's absorption of a 70s' aesthetic. This aesthetic – lots of oranges and browns and a washed-out look – actually reflected the memories of an audience reared on faded prints of 70s' film stock and harshly lit TV studio work in the years since. *Life on Mars* acknowledges the complexity and fascination of the 70s in a way unimaginable a decade earlier but is very much a view from hindsight, a guide to understanding how the 70s leads to today.

31

Another look at the decade in hindsight is of great interest here. In 2005, the BBC screened a TV serialisation of Jonathan Coe's novel about growing up in Birmingham in the 1970s, *The Rotters' Club*, adapted by none other than Dick Clement and Ian La Frenais. *Whatever Happened to the Likely Lads?* grapples with the times as they happened, capturing the bewilderment of ordinary people benefiting from, but also threatened by, very rapid social and economic changes. In *The Rotters' Club*, Clement and La Frenais reappraised the period from the distance of thirty years.

In recreating the period in 2005 they had to take account of a new audience who weren't there or were too young to remember that time. They were also adapting the work of Coe, a man of a different generation (born 1961, so equivalent in age to the adolescent heroes of his novel) and from a different place (Birmingham, not Newcastle or London). When I spoke to Clement and La Frenais they were very enthusiastic about the experience of *The Rotters' Club*, not least because, as La Frenais explained, it went on from the familiar territory of the early 70s to later in the decade, including the strikes at the Longbridge car plant and the rise of punk. Ironically, these were their 'missing years'; newly in America and unable to leave if they wanted to retain their green cards, 'we were removed and Jonathan's book reminded us of that period'.[46]

Revisiting the 70s is informed by the memory of shows like *Whatever Happened to the Likely Lads?*, relying on their reference points for the audience. The series is so in tune with the nuances of its age it gives weight and meaning to exercises in nostalgia.[47]

Whatever Happened to the Likely Lads? is bound up in the times, but also in a particular place. Part of the difference between the programme and *The Rotters' Club* reflects the different experiences in different parts of England; the 60s and 70s for Birmingham was not the same as for Tyneside. The 60s' series was ambiguous in its setting, emulating more the unspecific 'Northerness' of the New Wave.[48] As La Frenais has pointed out, however, the 70s' incarnation was proudly, unequivocally Tyneside,[49] and with a new facility to do location filming it 'became very much a North Eastern show'.[50]

Distanced by geography from metropolitan anonymity and wealth, Tyneside is industrial but firmly provincial with all that implies; both good and bad. Challenged by Terry in one of his more revolutionary moments, that 'his attitudes are so provincial', in 'Count Down', Bob defends himself by saying, 'I am provincial, I live in the provinces … would you like me to have an Albanian attitude?' The provincial experience is one that millions share but is often ignored by art and the media. If examined, it is frequently in terms of social problems; the humdrum everyday weft and weave of provincial life is often dismissed. This is the milieu of *The Likely Lads* and in part explains its insights.

The provincial experience is slightly different wherever you go. Newcastle and Tyneside has its own very specific identity, its own self-image and its own role in the national consciousness. Its culture has been reflected too, in a number of popular works that have emphasised particular aspects of the Geordie world.

The North East as a region has long been seen as 'different' from the rest of England. When *The Likely Lads* started to screen, this difference had recently been emphasised. After reports highlighting poverty on Tyneside appeared in 1962 there was a period of ostentatious activity in the area by the then Conservative government, involving frequent trips by Quentin Hogg and the establishment of a regional development agency.[51] While some of the 'never had it so good prosperity' was enjoyed by some skilled workers, like Bob and Terry, the region was lagging behind overall, highlighted by an unemployment rate of 8.8 per cent against a national average of 2.2 per cent.

In 1964 the journalist Geoffrey Moorhouse travelled around the country to write a book, *Britain in the Sixties: The Other England*. In Newcastle he discovers 'the musty taint of poverty' and 'more poverty than any other part of England', yet he also detects optimism for times to come, 'the feel of an area which is about to move ahead in a big way after years of marking time'.[52] He notes that this growing feeling of modernity is coupled with a fierce sense of regional cultural pride, quoting a survey by *The Economist* arguing that the area needs to be

33

'brought into the gin and tonic belt and out of the brown ale era' and remarking that 'gin and tonics would be a form of regional suicide as many North Easterners see it'.[53] The brown ale v gin and tonic battles, of course, predict many a Bob and Terry squabble.

Modernity has taken its own form in the North East, often instigated by local councils and entrepreneurs, and seen in symbols as diverse as the Metro Shopping Centre, the 'blade of light' millennium bridge and Anthony Gormley's monumental 'Angel of the North' sculpture. This has not always been for the best; in the 60s, T. Dan Smith's Labour council regime notoriously became mired in corruption over system-building new high-rise blocks to replace the old Victorian slums.[54]

The excitement at the possibilities of the area changing and becoming prosperous can also be seen in Bob's new house on the Elm Lodge housing estate. Gone are the old terraced streets under the shadows of the docks; instead scores of box-like but clean and comfortable identical semi-detached homes cover the land. Visiting the real house in Killingworth in 2007, it feels strangely untransformed over thirty-five years. Agincourt and the estate still feel new, just over the road from a vast retail park and an artificial lake. The house represents a summit of Bob's aspirations – the reward for years of hard graft. The opening scene of *Whatever Happened to the Likely Lads?* graphically demonstrates this. Bob and Thelma watch slides of the building work saying things like 'Look! The damp course!'. Bob delights in saying how proud he is; 'My house', 'Chez nous', 'Come round to our house'.

Tyneside culture is a source of pride, although, like other regional cultures (Liverpool is perhaps the nearest equivalent), it has a clichéd public face easily stereotyped by those outside – in this case pigeons, whippets, brown ale, Newcastle United Football Club, Gazza and Ant and Dec. However, there have been a number of significant works that have dissected this culture and explored both its distinctiveness and its problems.

There was a New Wave voice from Tyneside, but in literary fiction. As the novel was never filmed it is less well known than others but, recently reissued, Sid Chaplin's terrific *The Day of the Sardine* shows the experience of working-class life there at the dawn of the 60s. His teenage hero Arthur Haggerston inhabits a harsh world of gang rucks, alleyway fumbles, domestic squabbles and relentless, back-breaking, monotonous work. Arthur is trapped, pinned down by his world. At the end, still not eighteen, he is in an existential fog to rival Camus, terrified that his life is mapped out already with nothing he can do about it.

In 1996, the BBC broadcast Peter Flannery's epic serial *Our Friends in the North* detailing the lives of four Tynesiders from 1964 (that year again) to the present day. Newcastle forms the backdrop to thirty years of social and political history, taking in a thinly veiled dramatisation of T. Dan Smith's rise and fall, the miners' strike and urban renewal, and the leisure economy. Flannery's four main protagonists – political firebrand Nicky, concerned mother Mary, doomed Geordie and the irrepressible, but none too bright, businessman Tosker – live their lives alongside Bob and Terry but are much more directly caught up in political change. Our heroes are affected just as much, but less obviously have the hand of history on their shoulder. The two programmes form interesting companion pieces, one serious and one comic, about the effects of social change on ordinary lives, and a very distinctive place.

Another harsh look at the region and its culture – 1971's film *Get Carter* – has proved one of British cinema's most enduring testimonies to the seamy side of British working-class life. Both the dark side of the 70s and of Tyneside are exposed in Mike Hodges' brutally brilliant account of Newcastle turned London gangster Jack Carter's homecoming to avenge his brother's death. Newcastle in the film is a sour mix of the worst of the old and the new – Moorhouse's 'musty taint of poverty' is in every shot of the boozers, bridges, bingo halls and betting shops, populated by beaten, brutalised people like Albert and Margaret, killed by Carter for their betrayal of his brother for personal gain. No sentimentalising of the working class here. Similarly, though, the bright, shiny world rising

35

up in place of brown ale and back-to-backs is full of corruption. The gangster businessmen Brumby and Kinnear, with their gin and tonics and new multi-storey car park developments, are just as rotten, violent and ruthless. In this world the new prosperity is just an excuse to line their own pockets, the new sexual revolution just an excuse to corrupt young girls for profit. It is a nightmare vision of a time and place; a place that seems both utterly desolate and decrepit and soullessly modern and corrupt.

Clement and La Frenais have, of course, contributed to the culture of Tyneside themselves, not just through *Whatever Happened to the Likely Lads?* but also through *Auf Wiedersehen Pet*. Their view of the place, and of its people, is a much gentler, more humane one than seen in *Get Carter*, but it would be a mistake to think that their Tyneside was a totally different land. When Bob and Terry explore the slum clearances in 'Moving On' there is no attempt to hide the bleakness of the landscape's past, present, or, indeed, future.

This connection to the grimness of *Get Carter* is strongest in the film version of *The Likely Lads*. The location shooting gives it a similar aesthetic to *Carter* and serves to distance us more from the

Get Carter's desolation

'The musty taint of poverty'

characters. While it is explored in a subtler and more comic way, the realities of a culture built on machismo, alcohol, misogyny and violence are still something we are made to engage with as viewers. The block of flats where Terry and his family have been rehoused is already a dangerous slum and even the Northumberland countryside is shown as rainswept and tortuous, as Terry is dragged, kicking and screaming, by his Finnish girlfriend (Mary Tamm) to see Hadrian's Wall ('It's only a wall, woman'). There is something harsher about the lads too; deprived of the warmth of the studio interiors and TV's head-and-shoulder shots of Bob and Terry together at the pub, they become figures in a ruined landscape. Bob's mid-life crisis makes him bitter and spiteful, while Terry's faults shine even brighter. It's not quite Carter's world but it is one he would recognise.

37

If Bob and Terry are defined by their time and the place they live in and come from, they are also defined by class. They are only too aware of this; indeed, there are few more complex and comprehensive discussions of the subtleties and realities of class on British television than *The Likely Lads*. To some extent, the whole basis of the series is built on the question of class; conflict and comedy arises from Bob and

The rise of modernity: Terry's new high-rise block in the film

Terry's different approach to who they are. They, and indeed the rest of the characters, constantly gnaw at the issue, exploring its implications and what it might say about them.

To the British, class is coded through economics, politics, family and culture, recognisable in the choices we make in what we eat, put in our house, or wear. Arthur Marwick identifies its survival through the strength of identification with a particular social group – in the 60s 67 per cent considered themselves working class, compared to 29 per cent who categorised themselves as middle class.[55]

This identification is a subjective act. Are we what we are born into or what we have become? Do we stop being working class if we don't work with our hands? If we were born in a council house are we always defined as working class? If you become a self-made millionaire are you still working class if you eat brown sauce with white bread, or do you join the bourgeoisie the moment you have your first rocket salad and pick up a broadsheet?

Bob and Terry discuss all these contradictions and complexities. One of the most important bones of contention is the concept of class treachery. Remember that Clement and La Frenais give

Bob and Terry identical backgrounds. Both grew up in the same terraced streets with similar families, both attended secondary modern school ('cast into the blackboard jungle', as Bob puts it). It's not where they came from, it's where they are going that is the point of conflict. The debate is not between the working classes and the middle classes but one within the working class. Indeed, there is a noticeable lack of middle-class characters in the whole show, for Thelma is also of similar humble roots at Park Road Juniors; although her father (Bill Owen) has 'done well' and become wealthy as a builder, he still feels working class, a 'brickie at heart'. Only her mother (Joan Hickson) has acquired the accoutrements of suburban attitudes, dismissed by Terry in 'Count Down' as 'all the same that lot – the middle classes, especially those that have just been promoted from the lower divisions'; which says something about the limitations of social mobility.

Only really in a couple of episodes in the 60s' series are conflicts between classes shown. In the sadly lost 'Friends and Neighbours' from the third series, Terry's grandad moves in to suburbia next door to the Perrins, whose daughter (Angela Lovell) Bob is dating. While Grandad (Wilfred Lawson) (and Terry) are models of proletarian slobbery, ire is firmly directed at the Perrins, amateur ballroom dancers who chose the security of an office job at the Co-op 'over a few years of glory and glamour'. Bob, as ever, is caught in the middle, told by his girlfriend that 'You're a bit rough, Bob', and grilled over his prospects, while also being urged by Grandad, 'Don't let them corrupt you.'

The conflict is even clearer in the 'The Other Side of the Fence' in the first series. Bob is seconded to the office from the factory and his colleagues point out the gap between the two worlds as 'them and us' and 'oil and water'. Bob 'just wants to get on' but finds progress is not that easy for a working-class boy. He is the object of sneering from the car-coated sales reps and at the works dinner-dance is admonished for bringing a guest (Terry) from the factory floor. At this point, Bob makes a clear decision to stick to his own kind and tells the boss where to put his office job. It's a choice that he is forced to consider throughout the series.

39

'A modern day Andy Capp'

When Terry returns in the 70s Bob really has 'got on'. He is now a building site surveyor, with a company car, a secretary and a father-in-law as a boss. He has his own house and is engaged, with a wedding imminent. Terry, out of the Army, unemployed and without any such ascent, sees Bob's new status, and its accoutrements, as treachery. The wedding suit with tails hired in 'Count Down' becomes one such trigger. Bob argues it is merely a uniform, a 'suit of clothes' for an occasion, and will not taint him.

The new era offers hope for Bob's dreams of social mobility. The social structures are shifting with the consumer society, the decline of heavy industry and the clearing of the slums, appearing to mark a clear break between old and new. This can be seen in Bob's enthusiastic embrace (with Thelma) of the material world and the badges of social status. There is something evangelical in Bob's love of the new (and paradoxically his obsession with his life before he could have those things) that is both touching and a bit ridiculous. His obsession with membership of the badminton club and the long list of foreign holidays he reels off that coincided with Terry's military postings are an aspect of this mixture of louche confidence and desperate insecurity – so are his Norwegian ski-ing holidays (with failed attempts to converse with hotel staff in Norwegian) and his preposterous wine connoisseur poses in 'One for the Road'.

There is a long working-class tradition of mocking those that aspire to a culture and lifestyle outside it and there are elements of that here. Yet there is also a nobility in Bob's drive to better himself. Only very occasionally does he come over as snobbish and pompous, as when in 'In Harm's Way' he tells Terry, 'If there's a slump Terry it's due to people like you who are content to draw the dole every week to cover their beer, bets and billiards.' This voice of nascent Thatcherism apart (and to be fair it was Bob's money he was spending), Bob does not reject his roots; he progresses. He is supported in aspiration by other characters, not just Thelma but Terry's sister Audrey (Sheila Fearn) too, always an implacable opponent of her brother's view of working-class identity.

41

There are limits to aspiration, however. In the programme, those limits are trying to deny or belittle your past and your background. This is illustrated most clearly in the episode 'Guess Who's Coming to Dinner?', and a finer analysis of differing responses to working-class roots is hard to find. We begin with an unshaven, unwashed, Terry recumbent in his mother's kitchen with a racing paper and his sixteenth cup of tea of the day. A procession of visitors to the room – his mother, Audrey and Bob – tell him that he reminds them of that epitome of unreconstructed Northern maleness, Andy Capp, the comic strip character from the *Daily Mirror*. Retorting to Bob's jibes, Terry insists that,

I love Andy Capp. I'm proud of my home and my class. Just because you're flirting with the lower, lower middle middles; just 'cos you've got yourself an office job and your fiancée lives in a Tudor estate with a monkey puzzle tree!

Bob offers to socialise Terry, telling him that the old lads scene has gone and that he should join he and Thelma for dinner on Saturday night with Alan (Julian Holloway), a middle-class newcomer who works with Bob, and his wife, Brenda (Jacqui-Ann Carr), another old Park Road Juniors classmate, gone up in the world.

Once chez Brenda, we enter a paradigm of 70s' provincial sophistication, all vodka and coke, swirly patterned wallpaper and fondue sets. Terry displeases Brenda by reminding her that her dad ran a fish and chip shop, and she snaps that part of

> your reluctance to leave the past ... is because you haven't much of a future and you haven't much of a present beyond the pub and the billiard hall. Most of us have improved ourselves as people but you're an embarrassment to your family and friends.

Chez Alan and Brenda

Thelma denounces Brenda as a snob

Bob and, especially, Thelma wade in on Terry's behalf at this point, praising him for 'being honest and down to earth'. Thelma denounces Brenda as a snob and accuses her of parading her possessions in front of people.

The characters unite in considering Brenda's attitudes beyond the pale. To move on is one thing, to deny her past is quite another. Her shame at her roots is seen as a repudiation of their shared history. In these circumstances, Terry represents both continuity with the past and a measure of Bob and Thelma's current success. This is what we are, but also this is what we are not any more.

Bob and Terry's attitudes and positions reflect a perennial conflict within the working class, between the 'rough' and the 'respectable'. Bob is, of course, allied with the respectable. This was the case before he started earning more money and joining the badminton club – he represented respectability while still on the factory floor. This meant bettering himself; a belief in education, in working long hours and in caring about how he is perceived by other people. Bob represents a large section of the working class of the time, anxious to make the best life possible for themselves and their family and keen not to jeopardise their prospects of doing so by rocking the boat or getting into trouble. The respectable working class lived for tomorrow as well as today. It was a position that was tough; as well as being built on hard work and acquired skills, respectability was a status gained through behaviour, from a moral reputation. This always carried the fear that the badge of respectability might be lost. Outside economic forces could threaten very hard-won gains but also personal failings could bring you down, witness Bob's terror at being caught drink-driving in 'One for the Road'.

Terry in contrast represents the 'rough' working class. His life is defined strictly by the here and now. He doesn't care what people think about him, or at least doesn't admit he cares. While not a career criminal, he can be fairly insouciant about breaking the law. In 'One for the Road', while Bob is terrified that a conviction will harm his social standing, Terry revels in his arrest for football hooliganism. In 'Conduct Unbecoming' he is delighted to hear that his name is in the papers for a pub brawl. When, in the same episode, Bob is also hauled before the magistrates for fighting, he fears total ruin.

Terry's is a narrow world, with little room for difference or change. He is proud of what he is and the culture from which he hails – although he joins the Army, it is purely to be with Bob rather than to see the world. In 'No Hiding Place' he and Bob have a famous conversation where, to Bob's exasperation, Terry assigns one word condemnations of every conceivable nationality from Koreans ('a cruel people, much like all orientals') to Danes ('pornographic'), before admitting that he doesn't like Southerners, or, indeed, most people on his street. Suspicion at anyone who is not a Geordie working-class drinker and darts player stalks his every utterance – for instance, his initial dismissal of Audrey's boyfriend (George Layton) in 60s' episode 'The Suitor'; 'Hairdressers, Italians, people from Hull, they are all the same.'

His attitude is a curious mixture of rebellion, against what he sees as 'them', and conformity. When he returns from the Army he affects to 'drop out' from the rat race and refuses to get a job, thwarting the labour exchange's attempt to get him a position back in his old trade as an electrician. His rebellion may be, as Bob suspects, an attempt to avoid doing any work while he can sponge off his old friend, but it is also a rejection of the straitjacket of his allotted place in the class system. There is a genuine distrust of bosses and authority, but also stoicism about one's place in the world. Terry sees no point in aspiration because experience tells him that it will not make his life any better. Richard Hoggart considers these attitudes at length in *The Uses of Literacy*. In a situation where you have little control, people will 'adopt attitudes towards that situation which allow them to have a liveable life under its shadow, a life without a constant and pressing sense of the situation'. Rather than try and overthrow the system, Terry tries to subvert it by

45

'We put one over on them, didn't we?' 'We bloody did!'

using it for his own ends, that is the pursuit of pleasure. Hoggart goes on to argue that 'working-class stoicism is rather a self-defence, against being altogether humbled before men'.[56] Terry, rather like Fletch, Clement and La Frenais' old lag in *Porridge*, exists on 'little victories'; the bet won, the woman seduced, the pints sunk and the authority figure hoodwinked. When, in 'One for the Road', Terry swaps his sample for Bob's to get him off a drink-driving charge, he gleefully gloats that 'We put one over on them, didn't we?'.

Clement and La Frenais articulate the difference in Terry and Bob's positions most explicitly in an episode called 'The Ant and the Grasshopper'. Bob and Thelma begin the day driving to work early in the morning at exactly the same moment as everyone else in their close, before Bob drops Thelma off at her library and arrives on the building site at 8.30am. Meanwhile, Terry leans out of his window and admonishes the binmen for waking him up. Two hours later, as Bob undergoes numerous privations on the site, Terry, still in his pyjamas, picks up his milk from the doorstep before heading down to the amusement arcade.

Bob denounces Terry's 'pathetic existence' of transitory pleasure and is appalled to discover money he lent his friend to buy shoes being frittered on bets – and even more appalled to find Terry wins. Bob is paralysed and sick with anxiety over 'the sheer volume of things you have to do; study, go to work, service the car, claim rebates on the rates, worry about whether I can take Thelma to Morocco ...'. Finally, as Terry wins again and details his day of bets, beer, billiards and birds, Bob is forced to concede 'What a bloody lovely life you lead!'.

Terry's role in the series is always ambiguous. Clement and La Frenais, in interviews in the 70s, describe Terry as a 'terrible person' and say that 'I think he's awful', but that isn't always our experience as viewers.[57] I asked them the same question again and they were now more sympathetic to their creation. Clement said, 'He's not terrible – the worst aspects of his character are his resistance to any kind of change or progress', and La Frenais feels 'sorry for Terry, because he's come back and it's "What just happened?" and "I have no place here", so it's

The Ant ...

... and the Grasshopper

extolling its virtues and despising Bob and his fondue sets and spice racks, but it's such a defence mechanism rather than accepting that he's been disenfranchised'. Terry can represent the less appealing traits often ascribed to the working-class British male in his bigotry, chauvinism, violence and idleness, as well as his tendency to lie and sponge his way out of any situation for his own gain. Yet there is a lot about Terry that is attractive to us as an audience. La Frenais concedes that 'a lot of people like that sort of character because they say things in situations that you'd like to but don't [because they don't] care what people think about it'.[58] His refusal to let his pleasures be unfettered is something we might sneakily admire, and maybe we wish we could have the courage to not care too.

In some ways, Terry is a vicarious figure for a lot of working-class men, particularly those that, like Bob, were expending sweat and toil to gain a new kind of life. He is who they wish they could have been, the popular boy at school who never bothered and isn't worried about the future. Greg Dyke, former BBC chairman and working-class grammar school boy, admitted that 'we thought we were like Terry, but really we were Bob'.[59] These Bobs were conflicted; they wanted more money, more education, but they were nervous about leaving behind what they knew as well. Terry's lack of vulnerability to criticism is empowering, even though his class self-image is portrayed as something of an anachronism in the programme. Audrey denounces him as 'the angry young man, except he's ten years out of date'.

The strength of *The Likely Lads*' view of class is its honesty and its complexity. It does not turn working-class culture into a pantomime for the benefit of the upper orders, nor does it offer easy sentimentality. There is scepticism, for instance, over the idea of working-class solidarity (often more of a theory than a practice, as my family found out to their cost when my grandfather contracted TB and they were shunned by all their old friends on the estate).

For all their faults, Bob and Terry are intelligent men who can analyse their own position and possess a large degree of self-knowledge. Their frequent debates on class are impressive because both arguments are valid and contain elements of truth. In 'The Shape of Things to Come', the last episode proper, they have it out again in possibly their most articulate defence of their positions as Terry praises his deceased n'er do well hero Great Uncle Jacob;

> BOB: You're just like him you know.
> TERRY: I'm working class and proud of it, if that's what you mean.
> BOB: So am I.
> TERRY: Get away! You used to be.
> BOB: I'm no less working class than you. I went to the same school, grew up on the same streets, lived in the same draughty houses. But that's my point, you still want to live like that, you like the old working-class struggle against the odds. What you won't realise is that some of us won the struggle and it's nothing to be ashamed of.
> TERRY: You still lost something in the process.

It is a conversation about class at a time when a lot of people were thinking through these positions. As social mobility for some seemed to be available, as the old factories and communities disappeared, what were they to do? Through characters that viewers know and understand they can think through their own positions. This was, after all, a dilemma that affected thousands, even millions of people – who had always been defined by their class, and Hoggart's, 'local' and 'concrete'. As the local literally became concrete that definition was now fluid. Terry's answer is to consolidate, to take pride in the culture you have and preserve it; to fail to do this is an act of desertion because the culture, and thus oneself, will become weakened. Bob's argument is that you should try and make the best of your life, for yourself and your family. Aspiration will bring material improvements, the basis of working-class agitation for so long. In his analysis, the needs of progress override the continuity of the culture, although that culture is still a part of defining your past.

My family, like many others, followed Bob's road at this point. Our material lives improved but we did not become classless. However,

49

our working-class roots became just that, roots, something from which you came, that informed the way you were but were no longer part of our present reality as we took on aspects of middle-class culture too. For many others, material comforts have never appeared, and privations have continued.

However, something has definitely changed since the early 70s; a change that Clement and La Frenais seemed to sense coming. In retrospect, the series is an elegy for the old industrial working-class life, a life that had plenty wrong with it – hard, unfulfilling graft, poverty, narrow-mindedness, suffocating conformity – but also had vibrancy and purpose. For all its faults it was a rich culture that gave strength to people. In the 60s and even in the early 70s, as things began to go wrong, it was a culture supported by power; the British working class had 'greater power and influence than that in any other country in the world'.[60] *The Likely Lads* details this culture and *Whatever Happened to the Likely Lads?* captures it at the moment it begins to be literally swept away, as slump and recession close the factories and shipyards, and rebuilding and relocating demolished the communities that sustained the culture.

It was to get worse, much worse, as English working-class communities continued in inexorable decline. *Our Friends in the North* is acute in addressing the disintegration of the values, as well as the places, of the working-class North East. The split between Bob and Terry becomes an abyss in the 80s, one part of the old, majority working class bought off with mock-Georgian starter homes and satellite telly while the rest were stripped of their old powers and pushed towards the underclass. The Miners' Strike of 1984–5 is an obvious milestone in the defeat of the organised working class, but as well as political oblivion as they were abandoned by the Labour Party they had founded, the Thatcher and Blair revolutions sought to dissipate the cultural basis of that organisation too.

However patronising it might have been, the view of working classes from above had frequently been an indulgent one, seeking, of course, to limit their power but also mindful that that power needed to be acknowledged. As that power ebbed away, so derision of the powerless became part of a new cultural landscape, a process Michael Collins describes in his polemic *The Likes of Us* as from 'salt of the earth to scum of the earth'.[61] In the first decade of the twenty-first century, the employment of the word 'chav' and other such terms of abuse represent, if anything, an intensification of the class war. The poor are now seen as some sort of defeated enemy, reduced to a set of semi-criminal stereotypes. Those that retain a working-class culture but achieve any material success are mocked too, laughed at for their tastes and lifestyle choices.

This has become a routine part of public discourse, seen in anything from broadsheet fashion articles to even quality television dramas like *Shameless* (Company Pictures/Channel 4 2004–). For all its good acting and writing, and I'm sure some reasonable insights into the realities of estate life in this decade, there are elements in *Shameless* that are problematic in the portrayal of working-class life in a way that *The Likely Lads* is not. The idea that just because you're poor you are perennially on the scrounge, the take, or the piss is a depressing one.

One of the ways working-class life has disintegrated has been through the argument that we are now a 'classless society'. Even back in 1957, Hoggart opens *The Uses of Literacy* by saying 'it is often said that there are no working class in England now … most of us inhabit an almost flat place, the plain of the lower middle to middle classes'.[62] Plainly, though, that wasn't true then and it is not true now. Most of what you do and say, certainly most of what you buy, and where you buy it, is still understood to be defined by class. This may be wrong but it is a fact. However, now, unlike the 60s and 70s, it is not coupled with an organised and powerful working class, nor a sense of aspiration beyond the search for fame and fortune.

The Likely Lads builds a precise picture of the times (the mid-60s and then the early 70s), a place (Tyneside) and a class at a critical juncture in its history. Throughout their career, Clement and La Frenais have concentrated on the pleasures and pain of being a working-class man. Interestingly neither is, or ever has been, working-class, but this

51

has never led to accusations of a lack of authenticity in their work. Working-class audiences have responded to the work and presumably felt the ring of truth. Clement jokes, 'Ian and I are complete frauds really',[63] but both authors feel National Service was important in developing their ear for working-class speech and La Frenais recounts his experiences growing up in Whitley Bay, a seaside resort attracting the Tyneside working class, 'All these gangs came down in their teddy boy finery and I was fascinated watching all these guys', and time spent in temporary work in a lead factory.[64] Authenticity of experience is often overrated in this context – if it is good enough it convinces.

3 'Ha'way the Lads!': Men, Women and *The Likely Lads*

The Likely Lads shows a slice of Britain transformed by the changes of the 60s and 70s. But something else is obvious when we watch it too, right there in the title. It's also about the 'lads' – being a lad, being one of the lads and all the pleasures and problems that might bring. I want to examine here how Terry and Bob try to work out what it is to be a man and how they relate to other men, including each other. I will look at how the series negotiates the relationship between men and women, and how the characters of Terry, Bob and Thelma all add different perspectives.

The lads, especially Bob, find masculinity a minefield, partly due to uncertainty over what they are supposed to be like and how to behave at a time when old certainties and presumptions are being questioned. Amid all the other transformations taking place in the 60s and 70s, assumptions about gender and sexuality were challenged. First, the old puritanical strictures over sexual behaviour were finally being overhauled and, second, the male-dominated structures of society were identified by the growing feminist movement as oppressive. Feminists argued that women's role was as second-class citizens, consigned merely to supporting their menfolk and rearing children rather than taking an active role in forming society and gaining self-fulfilment.

Bob and Terry come from a culture that had a very fixed view of what a man should be. English working-class life was then thoroughly patriarchal, and the North East, even now, is considered a by-word for machismo. Even feeling the cold is considered a mark of effeminacy by the large groups of men clad only in shirts in Newcastle's Bigg Market on a January night. A distinctively male culture was established, centred on the rituals of hard physical work in the company of other, similar, men, the pint, the match, the betting shop and chasing girls. Interactions with each other and with those outside the group are governed by implicit codes of behaviour and expectations. These are unwritten rules that have to be negotiated; deviation from them is questioned and can lead to a loss of acceptance, and in this environment life can be awfully hard if you are not accepted. Rules might range from standing your round in the pub to getting involved in fights if a mate is involved. It involves a certain amount of 'us' and 'them', from not breaking a strike to hating another team's fans or another gang's members. It encourages a certain view of women, one that sees sex as a pleasure but women themselves as a threat to stability of 'the lads'.

Terry and Bob react to this culture in comically different ways. Terry revels in masculinity, in being a typical, chauvinistic, Northern working-class man; 'It's what I do best,' he tells Bob in the film. For the most part he is very happy to live the way he was brought up to do; to be distrustful of women, and of men from a different background to his own, and to live around masculine pleasures; to hop from bar, to bookies to bird. Episodes in the 60s like 'The Suitor' and 'Entente Cordiale' emphasise Terry's blokeishness and irrepressible drinking and womanising. Even as he hits thirty, he is getting arrested for 'getting his retaliation in first' against a bunch of Rangers fans ('One for the Road') or starting a bar-room brawl with an acquaintance because of a row he can't remember the next day ('Conduct Unbecoming'). Terry is not dissatisfied with this life, but it now seems to be under threat from forces like aspiration, feminism, economic change – forces that he can't control.

54

Bob is inevitably a ball of confusion. This is a culture he knows, that he understands, that he expected to be a part of. However, his aspirations to 'get on', to 'do well', as well as the changing times, open up other possibilities of what it is to be a man. He is also intelligent enough to realise that some aspects of the working man's world are limiting and unfair. At the same time he also finds a lot about that life attractive – going to the pub and the football, and hanging about with Terry is, after all, frequently a good laugh. Terry again represents the old life, and a conflict with his new world of Thelma and the attractions of the Elm Lodge housing estate. Bob is, then, the centre of this conflict in the programme; the masculine as the old, the feminine (in a number of guises) the new. This is quite a familiar position in the New Wave films that form *The Likely Lads*' ancestry; although I would suggest that the conflict is outlined here a lot more subtly. There is more ambiguity and sympathy than, say, *A Kind of Loving*'s picture of femininity as a trap of girls who 'get up the duff', commercial telly, faux respectability and new sofas. Bob is forever caught between masculinity as a kind of earthy, but dangerous, life force that causes him, almost in spite of himself, to have that last pint, to try and seduce his secretary, to throw that punch, as opposed to the forces of reason, which tell him not to be so stupid.

55

Lesbian feminist author Norah Vincent has published a fascinating book, *Self-Made Man*, which details how she lived for a year under an assumed male identity, Ned. She wanted to find out what it felt like to be a man so became part of a bowling team, went on dates with women (as a man), visited strip clubs, worked as a salesman and attended a men's group. She did not like being a man. She found that, 'you're not allowed to be a complete human being. Instead you get to be a coached jumble of stoic poses. You get to be what's expected of you.'[65] Vincent becomes very sympathetic to the problems of manhood and its conflicts, hardships and occasionally its pleasures. Initially worried about being 'caught' in her deception, she found that, 'I passed in a man's world not because my mask was so real but because the world of men was a masked ball.'[66] This offers an echo of the feminist theories of Mary Ann Doane, who argued that women were forced into a

masquerade to operate in society.[67] Bob and Terry prove to be adept
guides in exploring this masculine masquerade.

Over their career, Clement and La Frenais have been
particularly adept at shining a light on the relationships between men. In
Porridge we are presented with an all-male environment in prison; a
place involving a non-stop set of complex negotiations between men to
ensure self-preservation. *Auf Wiedersehen Pet* shows a less rigid, but
almost as fraught, masculine world of builders far from home, where
quasi-military rules of comradeship apply. In *The Likely Lads*, many of
the same rules, codes and impulses prevail. In all these shows, Clement
and La Frenais help us to understand the pleasures of male company but
do not shy away from showing its problems, limitations and, in the long
term, its ill effects. Looking at the relationship between two particular
men intensifies this if anything. As the series is about 'Bob and Terry' as
a pair, over ten years with a previous history inferred, it can show male
friendship, warts and all.

Eve Sedgwick has defined the world of non-sexual relations
between men as 'homosocial' interactions.[68] In the lad's world this takes
on a number of guises. There are 'the lads' – the crowd, the fellas down
the pub, at the club, on the factory floor. They are nominally on your
side, but your knowledge of each other is strictly limited and these limits
are agreed. Your connection is a shared place or interest, nothing more,
but you are expected to see them as an asset, and see yourself as part of
this shared experience.

Then there are your 'mates' – a group that can vary in size, but
comprises the other males you choose to see regularly. You know a bit
more about them, their family, their domestic circumstances, maybe
their misadventures. But you don't know everything; you don't know
how they feel much of the time and probably know more about their
views on Newcastle United's midfield than on their marriage or their
career. You don't even really know how they really feel about you.

Then there is your 'best mate'. This has a particular status and
function that is understood. It comes from a long, shared history and it is
not generally something that can, or should, change. You just develop a

'best mate' and that's that. When Bob and Terry meet each other again in the darkness of a power cut in 'Strangers on a Train', Bob tells the story of his original parting from Terry. He prefaces it to the supposed stranger with 'I had this mate – well, my best mate, you know'. The rules are understood.

In the 60s' series, Bob and Terry as best mates is a fixture. Their workmates express surprise when one is seen without the other. They have other mates too; mates that might be a bit different to them, such as the older Jack (Donald McKillop) and Cloughy (Bartlett Mullins) with whom they share their workshop. They have mates of their own age also, and there is a wider group of 'lads', men who are in the same position as them. You don't necessarily like all the lads, but you throw your lot in with them by working alongside them, or coming from the same street, or supporting the same team. There is the recurring figure of Blakey (Richard Moore), an oafish colleague who creates embarrassing situations and is utterly untrustworthy. In 'Chance of a Lifetime' the factory has a whip round when they think Bob and Terry are emigrating to Australia. The money is pocketed by Blakey, but, despite his deception and the fact that they don't even like him, he remains one of the lads through the exigencies of time and place.

Bob and Terry met on the first day of school when they were five years old and their status as best mates was cemented early. School together (in the 'blackboard jungle', remember), work together, even joining up together. When they meet again the relationship is immediately seen as an intractable fact, despite the lack of contact between them over the last few years and the bad blood of their parting. It is seen as a kind of natural law, challenged only by the prospect of Bob's impending marriage.

Having a 'best mate' is not seen as entirely a blessing, however. The role does allow a bit more intimacy than one can receive from the 'mates' or 'the lads', but it does not imply unconditional love or loyalty and its pleasures come with limitations.

The series shows Bob and Terry's closeness is built on competitiveness. In 'The Great Race' their bike ride to Berwick is an excuse for outrageous cheating and sabotage as both determine to beat the other. In some 60s' episodes they compete desperately for women. 'Brief Encounter' sees them unwittingly date the same woman, who has to endure their different courting techniques, and in 'Anchors Aweigh' a Norfolk boating holiday sees them constantly trying to deny the other their conjugal rites, motivated entirely by jealousy and frustration. In the 70s, Bob rejects Thelma's offer to put up Terry – when challenged by Terry that 'You didn't trust me, did you?', Bob admits, 'No, I bloody didn't'.

Over the years, Terry sees Bob as a ready way out of any difficult situation, always ready to smooth over the disruption he causes or to obligingly lend him ready cash. In 'In Harm's Way' poor Bob, beaten up by a jealous husband in mistake for Terry, bemoans that his supposed best mate is 'always the cause of his pain and anguish' and that it is he that reaps the 'consequences of your immoral behaviour'.

'Over the years I've carried you'

Later in the same episode, his wallet as usual the lighter for his friendship, he tells Terry earnestly that 'over the years you've leaned on me too much. Over the years I've carried you. From a young age, at school I always had to cover up for your truancy, you always copied my homework on the bus.' Yet for all this history of exploitation he needs Terry and can't really cope without him. At every fresh departure of Thelma's to her mother's house, he cries, 'What am I going to do, Terry?'.

Bob has his own inadequacies as a friend and Terry has his own genuine needs, beyond an extra round and a fiver for a bet. Although Terry talks up 'the lads' and lauds the joys of male companionship, he often complains of loneliness. For all the talk of his Army comrades and the procession of names of mates from the old days that litter his conversation, they are not much in evidence. In 'Birthday Boy', despite their good intentions, Bob and Thelma are only able to

Counselling – Bob-style

muster a few unwilling faces from the past to a surprise party; for the most part, they only vaguely remember Terry and soon depart when he inadvertently insults them. In reality, Bob is Terry's only real friend. Yet even he is not always a very good one. For all his loans and company, when Terry really needs him Bob can't deliver. In 'Heart to Heart' Terry, in love with Thelma's engaged sister Susan (Anita Carey), walks miles to see Bob and talk about his feelings. Bob is prurient about the situation, but is incapable of offering meaningful support, instead coming up with inappropriate banalities.

Often Bob and Terry's friendship is portrayed as a marriage, and a not particularly happy marriage at that. They are forever bickering and there are moments of betrayal and hurt. At the end of 'Moving On', after Bob has tracked a depressed Terry down in the byways of Berwick, he reacts with rage when Terry contemptuously rejects Bob's offer of a job. As Bob storms off, Audrey asks Terry, 'Why was he that angry?' 'Because he loves me,' is Terry's weary answer.

'Because he loves me'

Andy Medhurst has deftly analysed how the programme negotiates the 'shiftiness' between the 'homosocial' and the homosexual – the lads frequently alluding to the latter in order to ostentatiously distinguish their relationship as being close but non-sexual. As he puts it the series 'rummage[s] through the baggage that straight men carry', to show that the social can rival the sexual; to demonstrate the pull of Terry on Bob's affections.[69] This reflects the complexities, joys and even disappointments of friendship. Friendship is formed by history, by an initial connection like any close relationship. However, that connection can sour and, like a marriage that has mired in bitterness and resentment, it can carry a great deal of baggage.

Much of Bob and Terry's friendship seems to be woven through with envy, a desire to have the other's attributes, which they do not possess. It is like a marriage in that it has elements of love, elements of co-dependence and obligation, but also an underside of animus, and a sense of bitterness. They set themselves up in opposition to each other – Bob the sensible one, Terry the wild one – yet Bob wants to be wild too and Terry secretly craves stability. They don't just want to be one sort of man, they want to be all sorts of men. The strictures of society and their own failings seem to make this impossible so their friendship allows them to experience another kind of manhood vicariously.

It's not all dark resentment and ingrained jealousy. A lot of the time they have fun together and sometimes they do support each other. Terry's best man speech in 'End of an Era', a source of considerable anxiety to Bob and Thelma, is actually a rather beautiful moment. In graciously refusing Bob's gift of a photo album of their past times together, he tells Bob in front of the assembled party, 'I know how much this means to you, Bob, and I want you to know I appreciate that gesture more than I can say. But I can't take this kidder, it's about Bob and Thelma and Bob and Thelma only from now on.' This proves not to be so, but the scenes show that your friends don't always let you down.

So 'Bob and Terry' is a unit forged by history and circumstance, a unit impervious to change. They don't live in an enclosed world though; as well as other men there are women. How

61

'Bob and Thelma only from now on ...'

does the relationship between men and women operate? How, both in Bob and Terry's lives and in the world they inhabit, can they work together?

The fact is they often don't – sometimes men and women seem to be kept apart by a wall of Berlin proportions. Within British industrial working-class culture men and women often led largely separate lives.[70] There was not a great deal of mixing, even after marriage. Maybe a trip to the saloon bar together on a Saturday and an hour or two in the evening might occur, but in many families the husband would work long, often antisocial, shifts then spend their leisure hours in male arenas like the pub, the works club, the football stadium, the betting shop, or in pursuits not known for their enthusiastic female membership like fishing, pigeon racing, or model making.

Lynne Segal, in an article on men in the 50s, the era in which the lads grew up, reveals this world through examining studies at the time. She shows evidence that even within the home men and women's separation was 'reconstituted'. In a study of Yorkshire miners, she finds that 'for the husband to maintain his status and prestige in his social life with his peers, he must consciously distance himself from his wife and children, and be seen to do so'.[71] Sid Chaplin's narrator in *The Day of the Sardine* talks of his world as follows:

> the conventions are pretty tight … you only walk with a woman when you're courting her; after the honeymoon she's on her own while you go out with married men your own age. I've seen characters push a pram and it's held against them for life – they never live it down.[72]

Ian La Frenais also recalled a couple of incidents that shaped his view of that world. As a student temp at a factory in the (still) rough area of Scotswood, 'at payday we came out the gates and there was this huddle of women and the men gave them their paypackets and they opened it and gave the man a couple of quid back and they went off with the pram and the men went down the pub'. He also remembered at the height of the programme's 70s' fame going out in the city with Newcastle United's players and their wives – except that 'all the players stood over there and all the wives chatted with their gin and bitter lemons over there. I thought, I've gone back to Newcastle; I'm not used to this, it's not like trendy South Kensington.'[73]

63

If you were a man like Bob and Terry, you may have had innumerable dates but you did not 'know' women or vice versa. Conversations and encounters were coded and often you had to spend long hours in the company of each other's families, gathered in front of the only source of heat and undergoing stilted conversation. There was little scope for female friends, even though women might offer the insight and intimacy that your male friends lacked; you had to have 'intentions' to be seen together and then, as Chaplin implies, not for long.

You got married, you had children, but what then? Although marriage was the expectation, it would be wrong to imagine it was heralded as a positive experience for bride and groom. As John Ellis has pointed out, looking at the TV of the 60s and the 70s can be quite shocking to the modern viewer in its treatment of gender relations.[74] It is not so much that it is guided by sexism and misogyny (although it sometimes is), more that it assumes a state of mutual antipathy between men and women. This recurs so often that it indicates that this is what the audience understood to be normal; this was the way they believed it was. This antipathy, even hatred at times, was not just the preserve of men either. Certainly there is a view expressed by men in comedy and drama that women hold you back, drag you down, that they nag you as you work your fingers to the bone and stop you having fun. Equally though, as *Coronation Street* in particular still sometimes features, there is a female view that men lie, cheat, steal and invariably let you down and that they have no conception of your needs, desires or their obligations.

In this climate, marriage as constituted is seen as a necessary evil – one expects it to happen but one does not expect it to give you happiness. *The Likely Lads* reflects this attitude but offers a critique of its self-fulfilling doom. At various points, the lads express frustration with the way marriage is presented in their world. Terry may by and large support the marriage is a trap theory, but this front occasionally slips. He is genuinely appalled when Bob reveals that he had split with Thelma but decided to get married because they came up on the housing list. Terry is, after all, a married man himself. We never see Jutta, his Teutonic spouse, but his hurt at marital failure is implied despite his protestations and tales of hiding WAAF lovers in the airing cupboard. He is, he claims, 'capable of deeper emotions than the wham-bam'. Marriage is, however, still something that gets in the way – he may tell Bob that it's 'the end of an era' and their lads' life is 'all in the past', but still makes sure that Bob will be at The Fat Ox the night he gets back from honeymoon for a darts match. The rhetoric has moved on but not the reality.

Perhaps the most sustained and complex interrogation of this divided culture and attitudes to marriage in the series is one of the lost episodes from the third series in 1966. 'Love and Marriage' is one of Clement and La Frenais' most hard-hitting and savage pieces of comedy writing, showing up the miseries of this battle of the sexes mentality. The young Bob and Terry react fiercely against the pressure being put on them to marry by family and friends alike, especially as the picture painted is such an unattractive one. On being asked the question by their club barman, they pretend to be marrying each other with Bob sarcastically linking arms with Terry and saying, 'We want a nice little house – up on the new estate' and 'We're saving fifteen bob at the building society', ironic given his situation a few years later.

The episode takes place around the men at the club, interweaving the lads' discussions on marriage with the story of their acquaintance Duggie (Derek Newark), newly married to Bob's ex-girlfriend Helen (Helen Fraser). They express their mystification at why people get married, Terry predictably blaming emasculation by women; 'blokes we know – they get married and become shadows of their former selves'. However, Bob analyses the situation as follows: 'You take 99 per cent of the people we know – they treat marriage like some sort of battle. You hear them talking about "the wife" as if they were talking about "the enemy"' and 'Take the blokes in the club. They're always saying things like, "Oh, I've got the night off from the wife" or "The wife's away for a couple of days, thank God". Well what's that all about? I mean, if I'm gonna be so pleased to be out of the wife's sight for a couple of hours, why am I married to her in the first place?'

Bob expresses the desire to find an equal partner, someone he wants to be with and who wants to be with him, but this is not being offered as an option within the culture of the club. Marriage is seen as some kind of punishment that they can't avoid. Although the lads can see the contradictions and limitations of this mindset it is hard for them to wrench themselves from its grasp.

This is seen in the cautionary tale of Duggie. Duggie was a hard man; in a previous episode he punched Bob's lights out for dallying with Helen. Now, married, Duggie is seen by his peers as pitiable and soft for wanting to be with his wife and his child. His attempts at domesticity are disrupted by the club members. They arrive at his flat and ruin his and Helen's plans for a night in together, and ply him with drink at every opportunity to stop him going home. His attempts to opt out of the masculine world can't be allowed. The club goes on a trip to Morecambe; as all the married man get blasted and try to get illicit kisses, they encounter Duggie and get him so drunk they throw him, insensible, onto the coach back to Newcastle. When they take him home they find he was on a week's holiday in Morecambe with his wife and child. Any man's domesticity becomes an emasculation of them all in this world.

Although *The Likely Lads* is often affectionate in its depiction of masculine culture, it isn't here. 'Love and Marriage' is deliberately bleak in its satire. The grimness and narrowness of this 'man's world', recognised by Bob and Terry, although they are unable to see outside it, is also underlined by the appearance of a ninety-year-old man, Dan (Frank Cowley). Dan is a veteran of decades of club coach trips and proudly boasts he was at the bar every night of the war. As the coach picks him up, his wife cries, terrified he is on his last legs, and is brusquely shaken off. The pressure to be 'a man', and the very limited definition that entails at the club, creates a closed and cold world.

This idea of marriage as a battle continues into the 70s and Bob and Thelma's marriage. Much as Bob might understand that marriage should be a partnership, he is formed in a culture that denies that possibility. A pattern develops of misunderstandings, entrenched positions and recriminations, reminiscent of the attitudes he denounced years earlier in 'Love and Marriage'. Terry still embodies some of this mentality and Clement and La Frenais use the opportunity to poke fun at masculine delusions of superiority and matrimonial power in 'The Expert'. Bob aims to get back Thelma from their latest spat and relies on Terry for advice. Terry, here at his most maternal in the alternative marriage between he and Bob, comes up with numerous scenarios for Bob to assert his power over Thelma, all of which of course fail spectacularly. In each case Terry names a precedent, a mate that had done it before, appealing to a shared brotherhood of men against

'I am the master of this house'

women. Each time Thelma does not fall for it; when Bob tries Terry's plan to lock Thelma in a room until she submits to his supposed authority he ends up locking in the cleaning lady instead. Thelma locks Bob in as retaliation, rendering his entreaties that 'I am the master of this house' utterly laughable. Terry's status as an expert is equally risible. Marriage is a social construct that rules their world but is constructed without understanding, equality or love – in such circumstances the possibility of a happy marriage becomes a struggle. Dick Clement says of the cultural confusion that governs the institution, 'It was really just what you did next – really you only work it out when you do it. So many people go into marriage and they have no idea what it really means.'[75]

While *The Likely Lads* is a programme about men, and is largely from a male perspective, it does make efforts to think about women's perspectives on the world it depicts. Far more than in their subsequent work, Clement and La Frenais try to consider the battleground of the sexes, and indeed Bob and Terry, from a female point of view.

In the second ever episode, 'Double Date', the lads sit in a coffee bar, Bob mournful as usual about his latest romantic failure, while Terry affectionately mocks his appetite for love: 'If it's been "it" once it's been "it" a hundred times', and the telling 'She was coming between us Robert'. They perk up when two attractive young women, Deirdre (Coral Atkins) and Pat (Susan Jameson), enter the café. Pat is an acquaintance of his sister Audrey, so Terry sees a way in.

Both couples size each other up from a distance, contemplating the others' motives and strategy. Terry says to Bob, 'Have you ever wondered what they talk about when they are on their own? I have.' This is a key establishing moment in the series' approach to gender relations. Terry is almost wistful when he says this; he is genuinely curious but fully aware that he does not know the answer and does not

The battlefield of 'Double Date'

'Have you ever wondered what they talk about?'

expect to find out. It really is an alien world. The episode cuts between the couples throughout its course, alternating Bob and Terry's speculation and strategy with Deirdre and Pat's talks about the lads and the dating game. There is a symmetry suggested as the worldly and cynical Deirdre guides the more naive and romantic Pat through the male maze. As the boys advance on them in the coffee bar, she tells Pat, 'Here it comes, the take-over bid', and back home she predicts how the coming date will progress. The actual date is shown in a dizzying stream of still photos of them at a pub, a restaurant and snogging while waiting for the last bus. We rejoin each couple at the post-mortem, both pairs saying they enjoyed the evening, but giving utterly different interpretations of how it went. The lads cringe at an off-colour joke of Terry's they felt backfired, while a cut to the girls shows they not only had heard it already but also found it hilarious. Deirdre and Pat admiringly say that 'they didn't seem to mind how much they spent', while Bob and Terry are virtually weeping at the lightness of their wallets.

69

Again the episode shows men and women as somehow unknowable to each other in this culture. Their attempts to think through the other's motives and feelings are often woefully inaccurate and the strange formalities of the courtship ritual perpetuate this process. It is all about 'the masked ball'; relaxing and being yourself would be seen as a sign of weakness in either direction. However, 'Double Date' gives equal space to a female perspective, in doing so

'He wants to see me
again ...'

'By the cringe I've spent
some money tonight'

70

undercutting the male assumptions usually present in our view of Bob
and Terry's world.

　　There are recurring female characters that perform a
debunking function over the course of the series. Audrey, Terry's sister,
features in both incarnations as a powerful presence. Her position
remains consistent throughout, pro-Bob and his attempts to move on
and firmly anti her brother. Audrey is a strange mix of pragmatism,
ambition and stoicism. She marries her Hull hairdresser husband Ernie
(Ronald Lacey) only to find him a drunken slob and herself rearing
numerous children (including Fleur, named after a character in *The
Forsyte Saga*, thus flaunting her upwardly mobile credentials). She is
notable for her lack of sentiment for the past. Indeed throughout

sentiment is defined as a male vice, certainly she has no family loyalty when it comes to Terry either; seeing him as an archaic lost cause that drags Bob down – telling Bob 'You've got to get away from *that*' and praising him for his 'gumption' and 'getting on'. For Audrey, despite the iniquities of her own domestic position, life is about making the best of one's opportunities and she realises that women are not given them.

Susan, Thelma's sister who dates Terry when she comes over from Canada for Thelma's wedding, offers a perspective on changing womanhood. Affluent and engaged, she is not prepared to put her pleasure and feelings after social convention and family expectations. Ultimately, she decides that a relationship with Terry is not sustainable, but not before they have had a carefully contained fling and she has punished her mother for putting her in a straitjacket of Victorian morality by pretending she is pregnant with Terry's baby. Susan and her situation are presented sympathetically, rather than judgmentally, and represent a newly liberated woman that won't take second best – a woman that 'lads' will have to accept.

And then of course there's Thelma. Thelma Chambers is mentioned a couple of times as a girlfriend of Bob's in the third series of *The Likely Lads* – Terry angrily suggests in 'Goodbye to All That' that Bob is only joining the Army as a reaction to splitting up with her – but we never actually meet her. However, when we return to the lads in 1973 her presence dominates *Whatever Happened to the Likely Lads?*, putting Bob and Terry's friendship in a whole new context.

Over the years, in a strange act of collective false memory syndrome, the image of Thelma has become one of some sort of trouser-suit clad harpy who wanted to stop the boys having any sort of fun; a sexless, shrill snob who only cared about what the neighbours thought and whether the rouched curtains were clean. Watching the series shows how wrong this perception is.

Clement and La Frenais (and indeed Brigit Forsyth, who played Thelma) have expressed their bewilderment at this image of Thelma; the writers suggest it stemmed from Clive James's description of her in a review as 'the dreaded Thelma'.[76] They argue, 'We tried very

71

hard not to make her a monster. We tried not to be sexist very consciously.'[77] There is nothing 'dreaded' about her, other than the dread of guilt Bob might feel at his latest misdemeanour. Really, Thelma is presented as a sympathetic character; she sees Terry as coming between her and Bob but that is because he *is* coming between them, as in their more candid moments both the lads admit. So let's hear the case for the defence.

First, the accusation that she just wants to stop the boys having fun. Well, they still seem to spend an awful lot of time together at the pub if she does. Much of this supposed control is really in Bob's mind's eye, a reflection on his fears and failures of commitment. In a famous exchange from 'Cold Feet', Bob says to Terry, 'She's got to realise you're just a friend now, not my bosom companion. She's the one I'm working for and giving up all my spare time for,' only to reassure Terry that Friday is and always will be lads' night out, that of course he would still be at football, including midweek fixtures, that Tuesday night was, naturally, darts night and the regular Sunday lunchtime pint is definitely still on. Thelma certainly reacts with horror at Terry's reappearance because she understands that it represents a return to a mid-60s' perpetual adolescence and that Bob's self-image is hard to extricate from his relationship with Terry, the laddish avatar that at least part of him secretly wants to be. When she says to Bob in their Norwegian honeymoon suite that 'He's still here, isn't he? Even though he's hundreds of miles away, he's still here in this room,' she is right.

She doesn't trust Bob, but then we know he isn't trustworthy. What would you do if you suddenly found yourself unwittingly in bed with your husband's best mate, or your husband attempted to lock you in the bedroom, or strange barmaids entered your marital bed looking for male companionship, or drunken husbands turned up at your upstairs window in a borrowed fork-lift truck?

Time and time again Thelma makes an effort to try and accept the presence of Terry in her life, despite his hostility. An uneasy tension prevails, translated into Terry's wary greeting 'Hello Thelma – pet', always with a few seconds wait before the endearment that does not

'He's still here, isn't he?'

come naturally, but as the series progresses they do form some sort of
bond. She does come to a realisation that it isn't so much Terry himself
as what Bob sees in Terry that is the problem. There is reference to a 60s'
sexual encounter between them on a Blackpool charabanc trip, taking
place, as Thelma tells Susan, when she 'was going through that stage
many young girls do when they want to be mistreated by something
coarse and vulgar', and there remains the trace of an attraction,
developing almost into a kind of alliance. In 'The Go-between', when
Terry visits Thelma to beg her to take Bob back, he says, 'We've both got
one thing in common – he drives us both mad!' Their encounter at the
Christmas party in the special, where taxi driver Terry drives Thelma
home from an unfaithful Bob, is full of unspoken intimacy and shared
history, she giving him his present of driving gloves, while Terry of
course manages to wheedle a tip from his new friend.

So what about Thelma the snob? She is certainly proud of her 'lovely new home' but it is a mistake to portray her as a blinkered social climber throwing away Bob's working-class legacy. In 'Guess Who's Coming to Dinner?' it is she who leads the charge to defend Terry against the sneers of Brenda and it is Thelma who accuses their host of 'parading her possessions'. Thelma is comfortable with her roots and, unlike Brenda, does not seek to deny them. She enjoys the trappings of affluence and of status to some degree, but no more than Bob does – it is he, not her, who is terrified of what the badminton club might think. She is not ruled by materialism, and realises there is a world outside, down to her amusingly grandiose early ambition, revealed in the film, to be an ambassador for UNICEF in Morocco. Her career as a librarian is hardly the highway to riches either. She is intelligent, educated and prefers to use and enjoy that intelligence rather than make a quick buck.

So not a harpy then, nor any kind of monster. The problems in her and Bob's relationship are, it is made clear, of his making. It is his refusal to grow up, or tell the truth, that creates difficult situations. His expectation of marriage as a trap is not his reality, although he often fails to recognise it. It is Thelma, for instance, who often initiates sex and mocks the three pairs of paisley pyjamas and earmuffs that he takes on their honeymoon.

Clement and La Frenais say they 'tried to put her view very often'. It is true too that, as Clement says, she has limitations. She is 'hidebound by the vision of what she wants, and I think it's quite a narrow vision'.[78] She has allowed herself to be too caught up in convention and the day-to-day struggle, but that is easily done, and we understand her flaw in the same way we understand and empathise with Bob and Terry's faults.

All the talk of gender in *The Likely Lads* is caught up with a feverish, frequently thwarted, sexuality. This burning desire for sex is profound, poignant and, of course, often hilarious, as yet again aspiration and reality take a different turn. There is something inherent in British comedy that sees sexual failure as rich in comic

74

potential (consider Rigsby's face as he is spurned again by Miss Jones); desire makes characters ridiculous, but it's both funny and sad.

In the 60s' series Bob and Terry are overcome with desire every minute of the day – everything else is secondary to the dream of sex, the hope of physical fulfilment. In 'The Old Magic', when they reminisce about this period, they remember being 'that randy' and talk of their greatest ever season – 1965 'a very good year for blue-eyed girls', 'blue-eyed, green-eyed, cross-eyed ...'. In 'Entente Cordiale' they marvel at the teenage girls they met on holiday, in 'Older Women Are More Experienced' it's the late-thirtysomething manageress of the works canteen that is the object of desire. Even when all indications are good, their desires are constantly thwarted. In 'The Old Magic', Bob asks Terry 'I know we took a lot of girls out that year, but did you really have any complete, total, knockout victories?', and they are forced to concede that neither of them did.

75

No complete, total, knockout victories

There are also references to their points system of sexual success with various local girls in this period. Again it is clear this is based on wish-fulfilment rather than achievement, both constructing their own opaque systems to give the impression they were cock of the walk – in fact they are lying even to themselves.

Most people's 60s didn't really swing. Most people still lived very restricted lives and sexual knowledge was limited. Contraception was hard to come by so women had a lot to fear – not least the opprobrium of a society where abortion was still conducted in backstreets and unmarried mothers shunned. The codes that most people lived by, and all had to live in, were still deeply conservative. In such circumstances Bob and Terry, for all their youthful swagger and swirling hormones, were largely doomed to ultimate failure.

By 1973–4 sexual liberation has spread from its bohemian enclaves and is quickly becoming established in the wider world. With the genie out of the bottle there is a new understanding about sex and desire and an urge to make up for the years of repressive misery, and make up for it fast. The contraceptive pill came into widespread use after 1969[79] and women could now seek their own pleasure.

Somehow though, Bob and Terry have trouble adjusting to this new world, although it offers all they once wished for. At the beginning of 'The Old Magic', Terry is taken aback at the candour of the problem pages of a magazine, and particularly at the English small-town addresses from where the confessions hail. 'If this is anything to go by half the nation is behind locked doors in frilly underclothes beating themselves to death with riding crops.' In the second series he is also confounded by a sexually confident barmaid who makes advances to him on a fishing holiday. He is unsure how to behave, does not expect any result from his chat-up lines and is shocked when the barmaid comes to his room. He is still playing by 60s' rules.

Bob is attached, and left cursing his inability to act on his impulses (although he is sometimes all too able to do so). Terry is acutely conscious that the sexual revolution is not going his way. To women he seems unsophisticated, too redolent of the lights off, socks

Terry intimidated by the liberated woman

on world that they are leaving behind. In 'I'll Never Forget Whatshername' he tries to get back in touch with old girlfriends only to find them long moved on and at every turn he is bested by Bob, who is charming every passing woman with his bouffant hair, *blue stratos* and, most paradoxically, his wedding ring.

Bob's sexual chaos in the 70s' series is a source of both comedy and fascination. His sex drive is a force that seems to control him utterly, against his better judgment. Norah Vincent talks about her discovery of this in her year of posing as a man, saying 'male sexuality felt like something you weren't supposed to feel but did, like something heavy you were carrying around and had nowhere to unload'.[80]

Bob is torn apart by libido on the one hand and guilt on the other, and this dilemma, for all the laughs that result, is understood sympathetically. Bob loves Thelma and, as Audrey tells him he is a 'born married man', but is also consumed with desire for other women, a

desire he finds hard to resist. This becomes even more marked in the
second series once he is married. In 1966 he complained in 'Love and
Marriage' of his older workmates that 'they're always so much randier
once they get married. They can never take their eyes off other women',
and so it becomes for him. He finds that he becomes a more attractive
proposition for women now he has the allure of a married man. In
'Heart to Heart', fresh back from his honeymoon, he boasts to Terry of
his lust for the young secretaries at work and the 'spare in that hotel',
and is beside himself with anticipation of 'naughty in The Wheatsheaf'
that night. This actually stirs the rarely ruffled moral core of Terry
Collier who tells him 'overnight you've become a typical married man',
and asks rather touchingly, 'Why couldn't you have been like this before
you were married?'. Later he is driven to accuse Bob of making
'infidelity an art form'.

    Being married seems to set off a panic button in Bob that many
men would recognise. It is not his love of his wife that he doubts, but
there is a terror that a chapter has ended. This is more than just the lad's
life; it is the possibility that you could strike lucky, the possibility of
seduction even though it almost never actually happens. The reality that
it can now never happen fills him with terror and despair. Bob is
constantly aware of this conflict within himself and of trying to square
desire with responsibility and guilt. In 'Boys' Night In' Terry
accompanies Bob on a 'stag night' at home. As they go to bed (in a scene
reminiscent of Clement and La Frenais' masterful *Porridge* episode 'A
Night In') they discuss sexual fantasies. Bob embarks on an exotic
Caribbean beach scenario only to feel impelled to make Thelma the
object of the fantasy, much to Terry's disgust.

    There is certainly a whole new sexual world in evidence and
Bob finds it exciting but also confusing. He discovers hypocrisy all
around him. When the lads finds Thelma's father on a dirty weekend
with his secretary, Mr Chambers appeals to them as 'men of the world'.
Bob discovers that marriage and the sexual revolution will contain
temptations that he has to negotiate, and frequently that negotiation is
to cover up, to be deceitful.

Bob embraces the sexual revolution ... and Sylvia Braithwaite   79

Depressing though this socio-sexual landscape is confronting Bob, this is the way his world is made. The best demonstration of this, and of the new 70s' sexual environment, comes in the Christmas special. Thelma and Bob go to a fancy dress party and find 'happily married couples we've known for years – the lights go out and they swap partners and all that furtive kissing and buttock clutching goes on'. Needless to say, Bob proves that he is not above a bit of buttock clutching himself, with Sylvia Braithwaite (Lilian Verner), dressed as Joan of Arc. Thelma suspects, but in a weary ritual Bob attempts to evade detection.

In the film Bob remains torn apart by desire, desperate for both married love and sexual freedom. In the grips of mid-life crisis he resorts to chatting up teenage hitch-hikers and snatching a furtive romp with the daughter of a Whitley Bay landlady before finally coming to some sort of accommodation with his life.

So thirty or even forty years on, is being a man, and the relations between men and women, a wholly different experience? How much is *The Likely Lads*' take on manhood simply a product of its time; a snapshot of an age when men were defined by shipyards, pints of mild and Capstan non-filters?

In some senses much has changed; there are more women in the workplace and those workplaces are a lot more mixed. Certain offensive behaviours are no longer permissible. It is more acceptable for men to have close female friends. Marriage is no longer obligatory and the sense of it as a necessary evil fuelling a bitter battle of the sexes is no longer as acute. Have the confusions, doubts and desires of men changed though?

One way to consider this is to think about more recent sitcoms that build on *The Likely Lads*' legacy. Most comedy writers are still men and they remain interested in writing about the preoccupations of their gender. The idea of two male friends caught up in a slightly problematic friendship still has a good deal of currency.

Men Behaving Badly (Hartswood/ITV/BBC 1992–9) was one of the most successful shows of its era and became inextricably, sometimes unfairly, linked to the 'lad' phenomenon at that time. After twenty years of feminism, this sought to reclaim male pleasures – drinking, ogling and acting the fool – and put them into a new landscape. Simon Nye's scripts for *Men Behaving Badly* often critique this culture but tapped into the zeitgeist of the time. They centre on housemates Gary and Tony, united by their love of lager and their uncontrolled hormones.

The gap in this show is not between aspiration and authenticity and there is no real sense of class. What it does do is illustrate some male-bonding pleasures while undermining masculinity at the same time. Gary and Tony are crippled by the idiocies of manhood that they can't seem to sidestep. With Tony this is because he is fundamentally just a pretty face, attractive to women until he opens his mouth. Gary, however, is actually clever and funny, yet still feels obliged to adopt a set of ridiculous macho or boorish postures, from public

80

flatulence to drinking games. In contrast, his fiancée Dorothy becomes a repository of good sense by which he is measured, and invariably comes up short. Infantilised, Gary is incapable of growing up and does not see the need to do so; he wants a settled life without finding it especially satisfying and is content to bathe in the shallow end for the rest of his days, despite his abilities. Male friendship is a solace, but a pretty fragile one. Tony sleeps with Dorothy behind Gary's back and competition is always near the surface.

Men Behaving Badly, twenty years after Bob and Terry put their pint glasses on the bar, shows a limited masculine world where men and women still seem utterly incompatible. They think differently, have opposed needs and aspirations and don't even laugh at the same things.

Over ten years later a contemporary British sitcom, Channel 4's *Peep Show* (Objective/C4 2003–), written by Sam Bain and Jesse Armstrong, is an even closer fit to the *Likely Lads* blueprint. *Peep Show* places its two male archetypes, flatmates Mark and Jez, in a contemporary culture full of gender confusions and lets us share them through the device of hearing their thoughts voiced over subjective point-of-view camera shots. They are not defined by class conflict, both being solidly middle-class former students, yet they represent two different poles in modern male experience.

81

Mark is a corporate man, working at a credit company, wearing a suit and trying to climb the greasy pole. In this respect he has a resemblance to Bob, but rather than 'getting on' he is trying to keep afloat, conscious of the social expectations to hold down a job and give all your waking hours to meaningless reports and spreadsheets. Jez, meanwhile, takes a more Terry-like route 'dropping out of the rat race', but in the new mode of drugs and dance music rather than billiards and bookies. Jez is convinced that he is somehow free but palpably isn't, anchored down both by the weight of social structures and by his own tendency to be a complete twerp.

Both of them seem utterly bewildered by what is expected of them as men. They are roughly the same age as Bob and Terry in the 70s, but even more seem to be in severely arrested development, caught up in

Peep Show

an adolescence they are powerless to end and don't really enjoy any more. Mark eventually succumbs to the trace elements of the old social expectations – agreeing to marry his girlfriend Sophie out of embarrassment just as he realises he doesn't actually love her, culminating in a disastrous wedding ceremony that forms one of the most exquisite chapters in the book of British comic embarrassment. He is forever 'uncomfortable in his own skin' and terrified he is not man enough. Hearing his frantic thought processes points up the poignant (yet hilarious) gap between aspiration and reality.

Although men and women can now be friends they are still desperately confused by desire – Mark determined to repress it to retain some semblance of control, Jez determined to indulge it, then reaping the consequences as his marriage fails due to his infidelity. His liberation doesn't seem to make him happy and neither does Mark's denial.

Again male friendship is positioned as just a fact, something that just is, rather than a source of support or pleasure. Mark and Jez have absolutely nothing in common and don't really like each other that much. Yet they feel they are somehow bound to each other by history and rely, in a way, on the other's failure. They certainly can't trust each other; Jez snogs Mark's fiancée (and sleeps with his sister) and Mark's loyalty is more theoretical than practical, despite his much-vaunted morality.

From this evidence, while much has apparently altered, little has really changed. While the conformity of attitude and existence that faced Bob and Terry when they became men has become less intense, men still seem bound by convention and their horizons are still made to be narrow. They are still made to think about women in an objectified way, yet their desire is a source of confusion, doubt and guilt. As Norah Vincent says 'people see weakness in a woman and they want to help. They see weakness in a man and they want to stamp it out'.[81]

Jonathan Rutherford argues that the modern working-class equivalents of Bob and Terry 'cling to the traditional masculinities. They are chauvinistic, archaic, and rooted in the industrial revolution, but they have few other viable models of male working class integrity and dignity.'[82]

Indeed, there is now a model of manhood not so removed from the one that Bob and Terry encountered, the effects of which go beyond the working class. It is based around a limited palate of allowed interests and pleasures, all of which are commodified and diminished. Passion, now a thoroughly debased word, is now purely preserved for the Sky Sports screen at the pub in a miserable parody of male working-class culture. 'Passion' is allowable as long as it doesn't mean anything, whether it's love for women (or other men) or a desire to change society. Male life and identity is pushed into lager, football, *Nuts* and *Top Gear* (BBC 1977–) in the same way as women are pushed into a corner of chocolate, shopping, waxing and *Heat* magazine. *The Likely Lads* shines a light into the limits of being a man in a way that is sympathetic but aware of masculine absurdities and the restrictions put upon male thinking; it still feels valid now.

4 Having a Laugh: The Comedy of *The Likely Lads*

If *The Likely Lads* concentrated solely on exploring class, society and gender issues it would be an edition of *Panorama* instead of a situation comedy. Primarily the series aims to make us laugh – it is a primetime, mainstream sitcom that is intended to amuse a large number of people. Clearly, I believe that it succeeds in this aim, but how does it do so? What actually makes the show funny? Why do we laugh at what we are seeing and hearing? Secure in my belief that analysing comedy does not take all the fun out of it, it is time to enter these notoriously treacherous waters.

Sitcom – comedy that derives from a recurring situation – is, as Steve Neale and Frank Krutnik state, 'a mode of repeatable narrative which is particularly suited to the institutional imperative of the broadcast media to draw and maintain a regular audience'.[83] It developed in radio from the 40s in the USA and UK. Comedy radio reviews like *It's That Man Again* (BBC 1939–48) found the value in recurring characters that the audience could look forward to encountering each week, and *Life with the Lyons* (BBC 1951–61), a comedy based around the family life of American actors in London, showed the value of a consistent setting from which the comedy could operate.

Television expanded rapidly in the 50s, with sales of sets giving most households access to the medium by the end of the decade. Audiences familiar with some principles of continuing comedy from radio responded enthusiastically to seeing comic situations unfold on the screen and to a more developed conception of what a 'sitcom' should involve.

In the early days of TV, radio talent was shipped over wholesale to provide personnel, so the first major sitcoms on both sides of the Atlantic featured comic radio stars, like Jack Benny or Tony Hancock. It is Hancock that defined the way that British TV sitcom would develop in his shows of the late 50s and early 60s, written by Galton and Simpson. While the situation retained some of the looseness of radio (Tony's profession could change from week to week as the comedy dictated) it was Hancock's character, 'the lad himself', Anthony St John Aloysius Hancock, who sent British sitcoms down a rather different route to the Americans.

Hancock is a loser, a deeply inadequate, pompous, slightly pitiable fellow, yet the public seemed to love that in him. From this moment on, much of British sitcom has had a rather dark hue. Either it features characters that are less than likeable (Basil Fawlty, Alf Garnett, or Rigsby), or those that for all their good intentions were destined to fail (Harold Steptoe or Captain Mainwaring).

85

The humdrum settings of Hancock, mired in suburbia with his hopeless friends in East Cheam, and later marooned in the isolation of a one-room bedsit in Earl's Court, set another kind of precedent. British audiences seem to respond to the shabby everyday rather than to idealised luxury or comfort. No glamorous showbiz lifestyles or swanky apartments here. Instead, British sitcoms have relied on the familiar, the down at heel, for laughs; the factory floor, the suburban semi, the failing seaside hotel, the market stall.

Lastly, Galton and Simpson's success with Hancock, and later with *Steptoe and Son*, set up a different model of sitcom production to the USA. In the USA, the demands of syndication required a high number of episodes, more than one or two people could reasonably turn around.

Writing teams are used instead; tables of confident talents all keen to prove themselves by working to polish every line of dialogue until it gleams. Inevitably, this had led to a reliance on the gag, and the tough commercial environment means that the audience have to be made to laugh as much as possible to illustrate that the show is a success. In Britain there is no syndication and consequently shorter runs. Galton and Simpson's (and indeed Clement and La Frenais') triumphs led to an authored tradition where individuals or pairs of writers were responsible for all the scripts. British sitcom writing is then defined by the characters within the situation and the tone of its author; the scripts bear their mark in a way that is not usually possible in the American system.

The Likely Lads was born relatively early in the life of the TV sitcom in this country, but reflects all of these traits. It deals with low-achievers and flawed, luckless folk. It has the most everyday of settings; nothing glamorous, nothing inherently dramatic or exciting. And it is heavily authored; Clement and La Frenais have a particular style of writing that permeates the piece, a style we can learn to recognise and love as it draws us into being part of Bob and Terry's world.

Clement and La Frenais are not part of the postwar British comedy world, based around writing for comedians in stand-up, radio or TV variety, and they have no links with the club scene, the Goons crowd, or the Cambridge footlights set, the dominant strands of British comedy through the 60s. They do, however, understand how sitcom works, and how it is a distinctive type of comic voice, removed from these other forms. They recognise its relationship with an audience and how laughs come from anticipation, identification and resonance.

Most of all, they understand its intimacy. If TV is part of our everyday existence then it becomes a potent way to talk about that everyday life; the little ironies that can build up a realistic, but comic, parallel universe for the viewer. To be funny they have to have some sort of comic logic – something that derives from the viewer's knowledge of the programme so that our instinct is to think that, when faced with such a situation, that character would do or say that. Even sitcoms that deal in absurdities need to do this. For all its freakish events and bizarre manifestations, *Father Ted* (Hat Trick/C4 1995–8) relies on our understanding that given any scenario Ted will always lie, and lie again, to try and dodge any potential embarrassment. Inevitably, the lies got more and more gargantuan but still were anchored in this character trait and the realism of drudgery at the Craggy Island parochial house.

In their study *Popular Film and Television Comedy*, Steve Neale and Frank Krutnik consider the tension between comic verisimilitude, that is, comedy that reflects reality, and comic transgression, that which undermines our usual expectations and social norms. Their emphasis is primarily on the latter, on how comedy appears to subvert the expected, arguing that '*all* instances of the comic involve a degree of non- or anti-verisimilitude, that *all* instances of the comic involve a deviation from some kind of norm, rule, convention, or type' (original emphasis), although they also echo Mick Eaton's point that the comic conventions we learn create a 'familiarisation of transgression'.[84]

While comedy always does carry elements of transgression, *The Likely Lads* challenges their emphasis because of its reliance on verisimilitude for its appeal. Nothing seems fanciful in the show and it frequently verges on naturalism. This is just like real life, or at least one where we are slightly more articulate about our position, where we think of the line before rather than just after we leave the room. I would suggest that it is the reflection of reality and the comic take upon it that draws the audience into the programme, in a way that is much more explicit than other sitcoms of the time. *Rising Damp* (YTV 1974–8) or *The Good Life* (BBC 1975–8) use realistic elements but also rely on exaggeration in character and incident to a much greater degree – indeed, *The Likely Lads* really anticipates much later comic models, such as *The Royle Family* (Granada/BBC 1998–2000, 2006) and *The Office*, in its approach.

87

The comedy of *The Likely Lads* is, of course, in the script and Clement and La Frenais' structures, lines and characters inflect situations that could be ordinary, or serious, or even sad and instead turn them into something funny. First, though, a word about performance.

For all the glory of the words on the page, they need to be made flesh. Audiences must see words being said on television; our attention is visual as well as aural. This differentiates TV comedy from radio. The screen focuses attention on faces as well as utterances, and on movements and actions. It brings out the silences between the words as well as the words themselves. *The Likely Lads* has a cast of supporting players and walk-on parts but it is primarily a two-, then a three-hander. We need to believe in those three people, to find Bob, Terry and Thelma credible, to believe in all they embody as characters.

I believe all three performers do this admirably. All of them are straight actors rather than comedians. James Bolam is, and was, the best known. He gives Terry likeability along with the chauvinism, deviousness and idleness. He gives us enough to make us want to believe that Terry is OK; to recognise his faults but to grant him sort of credit for a kind of decency and, importantly, intelligence. It wouldn't work if we thought Terry was stupid; he has to be sharp enough and fun enough to make us believe that Bob finds him hard to give up. Bolam does this, thus making Terry's malicious moments all the more effective. There is a particular Terry smile – a hard leer of *Schadenfreude* that we see occasionally as Bob crashes to another defeat, a leer that reminds us that this is a lad who would split Bob's head open in the playground, and who would borrow a fiver to buy interview shoes and then put it on the 3.15 at Haydock Park. Bolam's look is just right too. Terry is handsome (if 'wiry') enough to get the girls, but also less than sophisticated. As Audrey and Bob point out, his look is stuck in a mid-60s' aspic, albeit without being combed and ironed in the intervening decade. There is even a great slouching gait, untouched by five years on the parade ground, a walk that oozes disgruntlement.

Brigit Forsyth as Thelma, as Clement and La Frenais acknowledge, does sterling work too.[85] Forsyth cultivates a splendid expression of slightly confused acceptance with Terry, suddenly darkening when she realises the full implications of the exchange. Similarly, there is the gradual raising of one eyebrow as Bob flounders into one ludicrous explanation after the next, before breaking down into confessional mode

Terry's leer of *Schadenfreude*

as he explains their new home is at risk of Terry. Her brisk exterior allows glimpses of passions bubbling up beneath – hinting that only concerns about what the neighbours might think are holding them back.

Best of all, though, is Rodney Bewes as Bob. Thirty years on, Bewes has rather taken on the mantle of a cautionary tale for actors; a warning to those enjoying public acclaim that it might not last. This has been heightened by a contrast with Bolam, accentuated by the saga (recounted by Bewes in his autobiography) of how the two Likely Lads haven't spoken since an argument just after the film version.[86] Bolam had great success in a straight role just after *Whatever Happened to the Likely Lads?* ended with Geordie 30s' saga *When the Boat Comes In* (BBC 1976–9). He has rarely left the small screen since, with roles in other sitcoms, comedy-dramas, such as the current hit *New Tricks* (Wall to Wall/BBC 2004–), and acclaimed serious roles, such as the murderous doctor in the docudrama *Shipman* (Granada 2002). Bewes struggled for work after the series and has spent much of the last two decades

Thelma triumphant

appearing in the smaller provincial theatres of England with his one-
man shows based on 'Three Men in a Boat' and 'Diary of a Nobody'. All
this has made it easy to forget just how magnificent he is in *The Likely
Lads*. It's a performance of astonishing comic dexterity, imbuing Bob
with vulnerability, ambiguity and, most of all, credibility. It's something
to do with the slightly chubby face and hint of vanity (in the 60s he
claims girls say he looks like Roy Orbison; by the 70s it's apparently Ille
Nastase) and with the eyes that express a gradually accelerating panic.
Bob's neuroses are given a physical manifestation as the jaw slackens,
the bottom lip quivers and the eyes plead in a puppyish manner for his
dreams not to be destroyed. The insecurity is also made flesh in the
slightly too pampered look, in contrast to Terry. The hair is just a bit too
perfectly couiffured, the suits a bit too tight, the ties just that bit too
flamboyant for a thirty-year-old surveyor from Killingworth. Bewes
physically conveys that Bob just tries that bit too hard at everything.

'What am I going to do?'

'It's so unfair!'

One thing the actors do not do is improvise. Bewes has said that 'people ask if we added things to the script. Not a comma.'[87] Clement and La Frenais' scripts are structured so that each event or line has a meaning within the show – saying something about the characters, pointing up an irony, or leading to a comic finale. 'Structure' of course has many facets in a sitcom. We can mean the structure of the form itself, or the way an episode is wrought so the strands of story are brought together in a conclusion. In both cases our writers are innovative.

There is a traditional sitcom narrative structure, characterised by Brett Mills as 'less a story, and more a sequence of comic events, with the audience offered a series of small, short-lived pleasures rather than the narrative ones which would be offered by a drama programme'.[88] There is a given, recurring situation with which we are familiar and to which we always ultimately return. The 60s' series, by and large, adheres to this pattern. Each week there is some kind of disruption: a fall-out over a girl, Bob growing a beard that nearly causes a strike, or buying a motorbike. By the end of the episode we will be back to normal, the old equilibrium restored. The last episode dares to break the equilibrium as Terry disappears in a lorry to Catterick and the Army.

In *Whatever Happened to the Likely Lads?* Clement and La Frenais do something quite different. The two 70s' series span a particular time period – in the first series it is the six weeks from the lads' encounter on the train to Bob's wedding. The second series picks up at the moment we left (and actually reprises the moment before), plotting the first couple of months of Bob's married life. There is then a gap of six months until the Christmas special and a few months more till the film. Unlike the old sitcom model, we are made very conscious of the timeframe – it is really a serial rather than a series. Certainly, it is important to view the episodes in the right order, which didn't always happen with subsequent repeats.

The abandonment of the idea of a never-changing world can be seen as part of the sitcom revolution that took place in the late 90s, along with aesthetic changes like the removal of the laugh track. *The Royle Family* and *The Office*, usually seen as the most influential programmes in moving the form to a new place, saw a progression within the situation – in the former, Denise and Dave got married and had a baby, and in the latter the Slough office took in the Swindon branch and Brent lost his job. Other shows, from *I'm Alan Partridge* (Talkback/BBC 1997, 2002) to *The League of Gentlemen* (BBC 1999–2002), built their comedy from the development of a narrative to the point that the old circular structure returning us at the end of each episode to where we started seemed archaic and preposterous.

Yet *Whatever Happened to the Likely Lads?* does this in 1973. There were the changes in Bob's situation across the show, but there were also events that begat other events from one episode to another. The end of 'Someday We'll Laugh about This' sees Bob punched by an irate neighbour whose wife dallied with Terry – the beginning of the next episode, 'In Harm's Way', features Bob sporting the resulting black eye and feeling distinctly frosty to his 'friend', who got him beaten up.

Within each episode the comedy relies in part on the careful construction of different elements, rather like one of those matchstick models of the Blackpool tower beloved by men with not enough to do. Each action leads to a consequence until we have a succession of incidents that take on an inexorable logic – a logic dictated by our knowledge of the characters. Take the programme's glorious return in 'Strangers on a Train' as an example. We see Bob and Thelma enjoying contented bourgeois bliss, looking at the slides of their new home. Commenting on their happiness, Thelma worries that, 'I keep expecting something to come along and spoil it', just at the point where a picture of a drunken Terry appears on the projector. The moment fills us with a joyous expectation, setting up an anticipation that Terry will enter their lives again. It is Terry we see next, returning home from the Army and heading for London, where we have been told Bob is going on business. Narrowly missing each other at a strip club defers our expectations being fulfilled, until we are gratified with the encounter on the train. This is drawn out to comic effect, however. Power failure means they can't see each other and Bob tells his 'funny story' about his mate who joined the Army to an ominous silence and an insult from a suddenly comprehending Terry.

93

A face from the past

They meet again

94

'Hello, Thelma'

Once reconciled, they catch up in the buffet. The reunion is awkward though, and quickly runs aground when Terry insults Thelma. Again it is all in the timing. Bob's admission that the engagement was broken off leads to Terry feeling he can speak his mind, only to find that they got back together and are about to get married. Bob storms off and Terry decides not to go home. At Doncaster he leaves the train and is spied by a waking Bob, who indignantly leaves too, thinking that they are at Newcastle and Terry is exacting some sort of childish revenge. Marooned at Doncaster there is something of a rapprochement, particularly as Bob feels the wrath of Thelma when he rings home. As the last Newcastle train arrives Bob gets on, then gets off when he realises he has left a barometer, a wedding gift for Thelma and his reason for going to London, in the waiting room. As he gets off Terry gets on with the barometer, emerging with a large grin from behind it to a shocked Thelma when he gets off at Newcastle.

It is a structure that involves coincidence and elements of farce, but is entirely convincing because of our knowledge of the central trio. We know that they would have those reactions, thus producing those actions. Bob's pomposity would mean that he would react in a wounded manner to Terry's jibes, even though he rather invited them. Terry would be tactless enough to make such remarks and is melodramatic enough to change his plans because the two fall out. Having established Thelma's antipathy to Terry, Bob's fear of what she might say becomes plausible, as, for that matter, is the idea that she might want a barometer as a wedding present.

The pay-off at the end is a recurring Clement and La Frenais device, used very successfully in *Porridge* as well as this programme. Sometimes, as here, there is a delicious inevitably to the denouement, but often they end an episode with a little twist or inversion that we haven't quite seen coming. Examples of this in various forms are Thelma climbing mistakenly into bed with a sleeping Terry in 'Home Is the Hero', the lads spending the day trying not to find out the score of a football match in 'No Hiding Place', only to discover it was abandoned due to flooding, and the fight between the two in front of the magistrate in 'Conduct Unbecoming'.

95

For all this, the comic gold of *The Likely Lads* is in Clement and La Frenais' words. Their strength is, and has remained, dialogue, an unerring ear for the humour of everyday speech. In the series, based as it is on the relationship between two old friends, it is the conversation of intimacy, of people who know everything about each other, have a shared history to draw on and have long ceased to need to try and impress or pretend to each other. That makes it different to the dialogue of many British sitcoms like *I'm Alan Partridge* or *Dad's Army* (BBC 1968–77), where, as Brett Mills points out, the emphasis 'lies in the gap between how they wish to be seen by others, and how they actually appear'.[89]

Instead, comedy in Clement and La Frenais scripts is often derived from banter, that strange male art of talking absolute nonsense to each other for hours on end. Banter can take on many guises in the 'homosocial' landscape. Among the 'lads' or with 'mates' it can be determined small talk on an object or interest that steers away from any personal information or emotional exposure. Sometimes this can be fun; sometimes it can stretch into tedium as infinite details on West Ham's back four, the performance of motorbike engines or obscure bootleg recordings are picked over. As Antony Easthope has argued though, 'the content of banter has a double function. Outwardly banter is aggressive, a form in which the masculine ego asserts itself.'[90] Thus, banter among larger groups of men can take on a sinister undertone – there can be a sizing up of each other, a jostling for hierarchy and a form of bullying disguised by jocularity. Clement and La Frenais pick up on this well in *Porridge* and *Auf Wiedersehen Pet*, but they also present the joyful side of banter in these programmes too – the quick exchange of one-liners, the witty retort, the understated aside of self-depreciation.

Easthope goes on to suggest banter also can depend 'on a close, intimate and personal understanding of the person who is the butt of the attack. It is therefore a way of affirming the bond of love between men while appearing to deny it.'[91] Bob and Terry know each other so well they are not jockeying for position, nor do they worry about what the other might think of what they are about to say. The guards are down and nothing is off-limits. This and the shared history assume an understanding of where the conversation might go and a licence to deride the other. This kind of banter is free to wend its way down any road, no matter how absurd. Banter is part of their relationship, a pleasure that keeps them seeing each other despite their differences.

To take an example, in 'End of an Era' Bob and Terry are in church as Bob prepares to be plunged into wedlock any second. Terry, as best man, is trying to keep our hero's morale up. He does so, conversely, by raising the possibility of divorce, claiming he has heard you can be granted a decree absolute by just writing to the government in Guatemala and telling them that that's what you want. He then mentions that it is best not to go there yourself because of their poisonous snakes 'that could devour a guinea pig in a minute'. 'But why?' wails Bob, 'Why a guinea pig?', before the conversation takes another turn, to the problem of venomous toads.

97

'Why a guinea pig?'

TERRY: An ounce of their venom could kill the population of West Hartlepools.

BOB: They've got enough problems with their beer.

The conversation, even at this moment of high stress, takes a number of bizarre twists and turns of useless 'facts', ludicrous analogies and understated ripostes, bringing the banter back from Latin America to local North East rivalries. All of this develops its own curious logic.

There is an interesting adjunct to banter that is employed in the programme at various times. This is the 'flight of fancy'; a spiralling of dialogue into areas of absurdity that take the speaker, and the audience, away from the reality of the moment through comic exaggeration. It is essentially a theatrical device – Mercutio's 'Queen Mab' speech in *Romeo and Juliet* is a classic 'flight of fancy' – and was much employed in early TV sitcom, which, for all sorts of cultural and technological reasons, was still rooted in the idea of the 'play'. Galton and Simpson are particularly fond of the 'flight of fancy'; Hancock and Harold Steptoe frequently go into extended monologues where they imagine themselves as someone else, or form a fantastical comic contrast with their own position.

As TV sitcom moved away from its theatrical influences the 'flight of fancy' receded in popularity, but *The Likely Lads* uses it sometimes, sparingly and effectively, to illustrate the lads' closeness and point up the comedy of the difference between fantasy and actuality.

In 'Birthday Boy', a miserable Terry strikes up a 'flight of fancy' dialogue with a stranger at the bar (Brian Grellis), a fantasy that serves to highlight their plight. Terry jokes that he is waiting for Julie Christie and Candice Bergen, complaining that 'they're always late, them two'. They both then enter a reverie about going to a grand fancy dress party on Richard Burton and Elizabeth Taylor's yacht. 'I like your outfit,' says the stranger, acknowledging Terry's scruffy attire. 'Yes,' retorts Terry, 'I thought I'd go as an ordinary Northern working-class bloke with no job and no prospects.'

Going as a Northern working-class bloke with no job and no prospects

Between Bob and Terry reminiscences sometimes spiral into comic confession, embarrassing memories sometimes proudly displayed because their closeness means they do not fear ridicule. In 'Where Have all the Flowers Gone?', the boys take an early trip down memory lane. In a scene later restored in many respects in 'Storm in a Tea Chest' from *Whatever Happened to the Likely Lads?*, Bob and Terry sort through old childhood belongings. Bob finds an old marble and gets into a state of some excitement. He recalls that he christened this marble Derek, because 'it was my favourite name. I always wished they'd called me Derek.'

Sometimes it is the words themselves – their sound, the juxtaposition of words in combination with each other – that makes the scripts so funny. Take Bob and Thelma's ski-ing trip to the Cairngorms in 'Some Day We'll Laugh about This'. Thelma complains about Bob's over-attentiveness on the dance floor with 'Morag, a children's nurse from Peebles', complaining 'I just thought she was a bit uninhibited for a children's nurse from Peebles.' This is funny for a whole host of reasons; Thelma's disdain for such impropriety, the thought of Bob shaking a flare in the nightspots of Aviemore; but mainly because of the choice of words and what they represent. 'Morag' and 'Peebles' are both redolent of bleak, Calvinist repression, so are all the funnier for being associated with louche behaviour, as is the saintly profession of children's nurse – it's no surprise Thelma did not expect inhibitions to be cast off. The combination of vowel sounds, the 'o' and the 'a' in Morag and the long 'e' in Peebles, just sound funny too, faintly ridiculous in their drawn-out nature and assumed seriousness. In 'No Hiding Place', Bob boasts of his stage career, claiming that 'the Home and Colonial Amateur Operatic Society still talk about my Nanki-Poo', and this is funny for the same reasons. There is a comic disparity between the seriousness with which it is said and the silliness of the words, both in their sound, like Nanki-Poo, and in the grandly monickered but actually resolutely humdrum Home and Colonial Amateur Operatic Society.

100

The words are also funny through their association with characters, characters we know intimately. Clement and La Frenais' approach to their craft is based firmly on character before anything else. They write together and act out the dialogue to each other; 'We're the first performers,' says La Frenais, 'we have to find that voice and then we're away … we've never been gag writers. We don't say we've got this great gag then construct something – we just write very organically and we're the first to know when we've hit a false note.'[92] This way of writing is where their dexterity with banter comes from and also that ability of choosing the appropriate word for the person they are creating; 'You always look for the truth in something,' Clement argues.[93]

Certainly, we come to expect a certain vocabulary, or usage, that matches what we know about the lads. Part of the fun is in anticipating what they might say in any given situation. This works rather differently between Bob and Terry.

He never talks about it

Terry has a number of stock exclamations that we learn to recognise. Inevitably, these are self-serving or dramatising – designed to shift the blame or get him off the hook. In *Whatever Happened to the Likely Lads?* a couple of these punctuate the series. The first is mentioned in that first reunion in the railway carriage. In an attempt to elicit sympathy over his Army career, Terry grabs his thigh in apparent pain, brushing off an enquiry about his welfare with the pious 'I never talk about it'. He tries the war-wound tactic innumerable times subsequently, often embellishing it further by implying he was involved in secret operations and served five years in mundane barracks only 'officially'. Equally, any time Bob remarks on the vast sums he squanders on his friend and his hard-luck stories, he is always met with an indignant 'You'll get your money'. He finally cracks in 'In Harm's Way' when he points out that 'You never pay me back', but there is cloud of doom over Bob which means he feels destined to always cough up the

cash for someone else's pleasure. Occasionally, Terry will adopt a
catchphrase over one episode – such as his maternal guidance to Bob's
marital problems in 'The Expert', where he is forever making tea or
cocoa and telling his friend to 'Drink it while it's hot', until Bob finally
retorts by pouring soup over his head.

   Bob's comic language, however, comes not through repeated
phrases but through his style of rhetoric. Bob's fatal flaws, his
pomposity and his anxiousness to please, inform long, impassioned
speeches where he tries, and usually fails, to justify his position. In
'Strangers on a Train' he climbs the high horse when Terry insults
Thelma, proclaiming 'It is obvious we have very little in common; I'm
amazed that we ever did have. Please give my regards to your mother
and father,' before storming off. Something about the final sentence
tells us why Bob is so funny – it is in this, the desperate respectability,
but also in the endearing niceness even in the depths of a deep sulk.

'Please give my regards to your mother and father'

This sulking is remarked on by Terry in 'Conduct Unbecoming', probably the series' most complete manifestation of Bob's oratorical portentousness.

> BOB: I'm not a coward Terry. I'm a man of reason, a man of peace. I don't fly off the handle.
> TERRY: You sulk. You go on sulking and harbouring grudges for days.

We know this is true. We have seen Bob's pained and hurt little boy look and the accompanying petulant silence many times, making his protestations all the funnier. The episode deals with Terry's altercation with local hard man Dougie Scaife (Alun Armstrong). Bob disapproves of Terry's fighting in the loftiest terms, proclaiming 'I'm a man of peace, a man of reason, violence appals me'; and when he and Thelma go on a double date with Terry and her colleague Anthea, he announces that 'There seems to be a modern trend to glamorise violence. I don't subscribe to that.' Needless to say, Bob's peacemaking ends with him beating up Scaife and ending up in court. Chastened, he assures Terry of his peaceful credentials but gets irate when his brawling victory is put down to luck, not skill, and he ends up fighting his friend. It is not just the gap between Bob's intention and action that is funny here but his overstating of his position and the words he uses in formulating it. The self-importance of 'I don't subscribe to that' has, in comic terms, got to lead to him taking part in a fight in which he viciously throws Scaife over a domino table when his nose gets tweaked.

103

Gerald Mast has said that 'tragedy is built around one kind of implacable inevitability: men die. Comedy is built around another equally implacable inevitability: men are fools.'[94] As characters, Bob and Terry can certainly be fools. They make mistakes; they get into misunderstandings through pride, sloth, lust and greed. The construction of the storylines, the words they use and the dialogue they exchange often work to this end. Yet they are not just the butt of the joke or of our laughter. Our laughs are not jeers. They are fools like we

'I'm a man of peace, a man of reason ...'

'You tweaked my nose!'

can sometimes act like fools and the series works on the understanding of this identification. There is empathy there as Terry loses another job or Bob is unable to control his wandering eye. Comedy is funniest and most powerful when there is a lot at stake, when it is derived from matters of importance to us, raising the possibility of tragedy even as it makes us laugh.

5 'What Became of the People We Used to Be?': The Truth about *The Likely Lads*

The Likely Lads might seem specific in its appeal. Its comedy might seem to be about a particular time and place, or for men harking back to their lost youth. I would suggest its appeal is far wider than this. Like much great art (and I certainly think it is that), it has foundations in the 'concrete' and the 'local', but builds something else on top of them. Ultimately, you don't have to be male, Northern, working class, English, or to have lived through the 60s and 70s to appreciate the show because it attempts to communicate directly to its audience to explore universal truths that most can understand and recognise.

This brings us back to the theme song. The melancholy of the tune supports the regret implicit in the words – 'what happened to you, whatever happened to me?', followed by the plaintive line 'What became of the people we used to be?'. These are La Frenais' words and, time and time again, right from the start of the series in 1964, he and Clement bring these questions back to us. The realism of the show takes on a new meaning then, speaking not just about the lads' circumstances but about elements of our own everyday existence. The heart of the show is in this interaction and the themes that it communicates – dashed hopes, broken dreams, lost chances, getting old and recognition of our own failings.

In exploring these ideas, Clement and La Frenais are melancholic but sympathetic. There is an empathy with Bob and Terry's dilemmas and an understanding of their elements of universality, examining that currently most unfashionable of concepts, the 'human condition'. Uncomfortable with the subjective inevitability of evaluations and the rigid emotional hierarchies laid down by literary critics like F. R. Leavis, critics looked to theories and methods that seemed to give a greater measure of objectivity – through structures, or signs, or through some kind of empirical research – to art. The study of television, perhaps mindful of the low status of the medium in highbrow circles ('We never watch it, of course'), has been particularly prone to this practice. The notion of the human condition thus seems to have been thrown out with the Leavisite bathwater in critical discourse. Robin Nelson has argued in relation to TV that 'there are many human conditions, so we cannot talk about the "human condition" '.[95] I'm not so sure. Of course the human condition has many manifestations and emphasis can vary in different types of cultural experience. Yet some things *are* universal, or we at least recognise the experiences in those around us – we get old, we die, we fail to fulfil ourselves. Moreover, we look to art to speak to us about these things and the resonance of seeing this struggle displayed through other, fictional, lives gives us strength, allows us to come to terms with them. A number of television scholars (including Nelson but also Catherine Johnson and Karen Lury) are now writing on the necessity of evaluation and what that might mean.[96] As viewers, we have no problem in conceiving of TV in these terms – we evaluate, we recognise, we feel, we respond.

107

This is what happens in *The Likely Lads* and is why I believe the programme holds up so well. Indeed, this willingness to get the hands dirty with the realities of our emotional experience is a defining feature of the British sitcom as a whole. From its beginnings, comedy has been wrought from tragedy and the audience has understood and appreciated this tension. Hancock is deluded and ultimately isolated; his is not a happy, warm existence but just a step away from despair. Paradoxically, this is what makes it so funny. We need to feel that we are being taken down a road where all that would seem to be important or righteous is questioned, even derided. Gerald Mast suggests that comedy has to remind us that,

> we are all human and mortal and fallible; that existence is irrational; and that we have merely invented the reasons that keep us going. In its underlying emphasis on the meaning (or lack of meaning) of existence itself, the goals of comedy and tragedy merge.[97]

Howard Jacobson goes one better in claiming that,

> The first and last challenge to comedy. If you are so clever and can do so much, make us laugh at death. Because if you can't, if you are unable to persuade us to go on laughing in the face of our universal fate, you have only ever been an evasion, a way of filling time not conquering it.[98]

We don't just seek evasion or escapism in comedy – it is not enough to be diverted from our fears and flaws, we need to be confronted with them. To many of us they can then be defused by recognising their universal nature. Seeing that we have no meaning in the world can become a strangely more comforting belief than that there is a meaning and we are failing to live up to it. The best British sitcoms have stayed true to this ambition; they have placed unhappy and inadequate characters and made them seem a reflection of our own failings. Rigsby desperately trying to avoid telling himself what he knows – that he is a sad little man and that even Miss Jones knows that; Basil Fawlty beating a car with a branch because he is unable to articulate his frustration any other way; David Brent convincing himself he is talented and popular. These shows dare viewers to take a look at a side of themselves they don't want to see. They can do this because they are comedies: if the same sentiments were expressed in a drama or a documentary they could be very hard to take. The payback of laughter is a licence to deliver these unpalatable truths and demand acknowledgment of them. It is a deal millions have made and understood.

It is wrong to think we are just laughing at characters in these sitcoms (or even at what we recognise). The audience is encouraged to feel for them; that's why Harold Steptoe's tragedy hurts as well as entertains, and why we were pleased when David Brent gets the girl and tells the repellent Finchy to 'fuck off' at the end of *The Office*. Clement and La Frenais are particularly adept at creating sympathy for their characters, even as they create more problems for themselves.

Clement and La Frenais' interest is in the weft and weave of everyday life, the legion of hardships that come our way with each dawn, rather than the dramatic grand guignol of black humour in recent shows like *The League of Gentlemen* or *Nighty Night* (Baby Cow/BBC 2004–5). In *The Likely Lads*, the comedy, and the tragedy, are to do with failure: the failure to be what we want to be, the failure to get what we want, the failure to take our chances and, ultimately, the failure to stay young, or to go back and do things differently. In focusing on this facet of the human condition the show is not just part of a tradition within British sitcom, but also within a much wider British culture. For failure is the great British subject, or at least the great English subject, from Tim Henman to bad singers on *The X-Factor* (ITV 2004–) to Victor Meldrew, failure is understood and accepted as an integral part of the human experience.

This is a recurring theme in English literature and culture. Thomas Hardy's heroes and heroines are doomed not to succeed, like Jude the Obscure brought down, rather than lifted up, by education, or like Giles Winterbourne in *The Woodlanders*, whose passions are not reciprocated. In the novels of Graham Greene or Patrick Hamilton, the central protagonists have made themselves marginal through their personal flaws; damned by God or alcohol, they lead desperate lives in which they are forced to confront their own fear daily. Philip Larkin's poetry famously relies on this concept of failure, envisaging a world where 'Life is first boredom, then fear',[99] while Morrissey's songs find strength in our ability to recognise our failure, without hiding from the tragedy of it and the terror of finding that 'a strange fear gripped me and I just couldn't ask'.[100]

109

All these artists (with the possible exception of Greene – but his faith is a harsh one that transcends but does not comfort) buy into Mast's idea of a lack of meaning, of 'illusory ends'. That does not mean they are nihilistic – there are grace notes, particularly in the respect for endurance, the ability to go on regardless in the face of failure. Rather than rejecting the audience, this creates a dialogue with them, helping them to come to terms with their own experiences.

This is what Clement and La Frenais do in *The Likely Lads*. The naturalism of the show, the intensity of our relationship with Bob and Terry that develops through the time we spend with them and the observation of the minutiae of their lives, makes the series a detailed and coherent study of what it means to fail. It recognises that this can affect anyone, but also that the pressure of life at the bottom, the inability to transcend an allotted social status, weighs very heavily. The lads are only too aware of the odds stacked against them; Terry accepts this, Bob tries to overcome it, but they both have been brought up with this cloud above their heads. Sid Chaplin talks about this in *The Day of the Sardine* – writing about Bob and Terry's world he says, 'failure hits the whole system. Worse if you're vain and look after yourself. Every time I got fixed on something easy this damn rotten failure would keep seeping through.'[101]

If we fail it is often because of ourselves. We cannot overcome our flaws, or our ability to talk ourselves out of a promising situation. In the programme, Terry's intelligence and humour is stymied by his 'forthrightness', which loses him friends and jobs, but also by the coldness within him that does not allow him to give. In his quieter moments, such as when he is a quandary over Susan, Terry shows signs that he knows he is to blame, but he also knows that nothing will change even if he tries; an even greater tragedy.

Bob's pain is felt even more keenly. After all, he tries so very hard – that, of course, makes it funnier but it accentuates the pain we feel on his behalf. He so wants to be respectable, so wants to be a good husband, to be what people would think of as being a good man. They do think that, but he isn't so sure of himself. He knows it's a façade, that within him are impulses he finds hard to control. He can't escape his background, and he can't escape his lust, not just for other women but for another kind of life, one that seems easier – in short, Terry's life.

That's what makes the programme so funny, this gap between what we want to be and what we have become, but it is what makes it profound and sad too. It does not take the fun out of it to understand this; rather it is that reaching for resonance that gives it its comic power.

Failure is dealt with primarily in the series through the concept of time. Time is the great theme of the show – it obsesses constantly about its passing, the effects it has on us and what that means. The passage of time has its own poignancy; it's inherent in the subject. We can bring out old photos and it can create a strange sense of both fondness and sadness inside us, through the disparity between then and now. *The Likely Lads* does this from the beginning, and dialogue and situations are imbued with a heavy sense of melancholy as the characters discuss or think about times past. Although it is a show about young men, it is there in its very conception. That press release that marked the first series in 1964 talked about the old hands at the factory saying there goes 'a likely lad'. But it is a bitter phrase – the point is that the 'likely' is ironic – the assumption is that, for all their youthful swagger, they will be brought low in the course of time like everyone else. In reality, they are not 'likely' at all; their dreams, their confidence are misplaced and illusory – very 'unlikely', in fact.

The programme is imbued with nostalgia for what has gone before. Bob and Terry are nostalgic for their younger selves. Their reminiscences are couched in terms of places and people they knew, but really it is about the possibilities that there seemed to be then. These memories can, of course, be rose-tinted, and those possibilities were not always at all evident at the time, but they are terrified by the thought that opportunities are now lost.

Dick Clement has commented that, 'What hit us when we were writing was that you didn't have to be old to be nostalgic';[102] while Ian La Frenais has said that, 'I've often been aware of a sense of change and a sense of loss. Even when they were very young, we were giving them speeches about loss – when they were twenty-two they were nostalgic about being fifteen.'[103] The flash boys about 'toon' are frequently to be

111

found, in their quieter moments, anxious about the inexorable march of time. In 'Where Have all the Flowers Gone?' the wedding of Terry's cousin sparks some soul-searching about their future and past. Depressed by legions of relatives telling them they are next for the altar, they retreat into thinking about the past, particularly the golden year of 1959 (remember this is 1965, which takes its place as a golden year in the next decade – most of their good times are spent thinking about previous good times). They root through their old childhood possessions and talk over the triumphs of their teenage football team, embellishing history as they go. The memories try to hide the limits of their future and the fears that their best days have already passed. Alarmed at feeling old when they go out with some teenagers from the wedding, they try to look ahead; but as Bob says, 'What have we got to look forward to? ... Married in one of those semis on the new estate and then your pension'; words, of course, that prove particularly prophetic.

Bob and Terry excavate their past

By the time we get to *Whatever Happened to the Likely Lads?*, time has become an obsession. Each episode sees some kind of exhortation of regret, usually from Bob, or a half-hearted attempt to come to terms with the fact of time. When they row in 'Strangers on a Train', Terry says, 'You can't turn the clock back.' They can't, but they try to repeatedly. Again and again, either Bob or Terry is brought low by the thought that the past is gone and can't be recaptured. In 'Guess Who's Coming to Dinner?' he argues that, 'You can't help thinking about the past, remembering how it used to be' – Brenda's jibe in retort, that he is obsessed with the past because he hasn't much of a future, hits home because it is what they all fear.

Sometimes the attempt to recapture the past is literal; in 'Storm in a Tea Chest' Bob finds it impossible to throw away accumulated rubbish from his childhood. Thelma labels this 'a museum of the 1950s', but proves equally unwilling to bin old hockey sticks and back copies of the *Bunty*.

113

'The past seems so much larger ...'

Bob feels unable to accept things the way they are. He has 'done well'; by the lights of Thelma, Audrey and the badminton club he is a success; but it is just not enough. He still is dogged by Chaplin's 'damned rotten failure seeping through', and he is tortured by the idea that something else could have been better. In 'The Ant and the Grasshopper', where the lads' differing lifestyles are compared, Bob feels broken, trapped on a treadmill of effort and expectation towards an unspecified end: 'One day, one day,' he cries, 'why do people go on about this mythical one day, as if in the future one day your life comes together and adds up, makes sense?' Clement and La Frenais are talking with their audience through Bob, articulating shared frustrations. 'One day', the demands it places on us, and the compromises we make for it, haunts many of us the way it taunts Bob.

The obsession with times gone by and the realisation that life slips away from us is, appropriately enough, captured most eloquently towards the end of our parallel world of Bob and Terry. In the final episode of the series proper, 'The Shape of Things to Come' (perhaps the best of all), Bob is suddenly confronted with the realities of his life, and of his past. He enters a long reminiscence about their days going to the Roxy ballroom, drinking gallons of beer, stuffing themselves with chips and trying to pull every new girl on the dance floor, before falling into melancholy about his here and now: 'It seems like yesterday but it wasn't, it was years ago. Suddenly, the past seems so much larger and the future's shrinking, and I haven't got time for the present.'

Inevitably, Terry accuses Bob of hiding from the past with his new life on the Elm Lodge housing estate. At the funeral of Terry's Great Uncle Jacob, Bob is faced with his past, present and future in the shape of the old man's childhood friend, Joe Hargreaves (Jack Woolgar). Suddenly, the past seems a trap, not a solace – seeing Great Uncle Jacob as Terry and himself as Joe, who bitterly denounces Jacob as 'a terrible man … everything I tried to do he mucked up'. Bob reacts as if this is an epiphany, saying, 'I've seen the future and it's a nightmare,' and trying to tell Terry that from now on he will not be swayed by his bad influence but will be pursuing his own course, unencumbered by the past.

Bob sees the future in the
shape of Joe Hargreaves

Bob's epiphany .

Their past is gone

It doesn't happen. The series suggests you cannot escape your past and it's hard to change yourself. The feature film is structured around a mid-life crisis in which Bob teeters on the brink of breakdown. Again, the vanishing past is the catalyst for a questioning of his present and future. He and Terry visit The Fat Ox in their old neighbourhood, having heard that this favourite old haunt is being demolished, along with the houses in which they grew up. Terry is remarkably sanguine about the whole affair, but Bob is distraught – distraught and confused. After claiming that 'these streets were ugly but they have a kind of beauty', he explains his decision to move away by blustering, 'I wasn't having my kids brought up on these streets.' Part of him wants to stay in the past, part of him wants to move on. He explains that 'the street coming down really upset me because it just reminded me how much of my past has gone ... in the chocolate box of life the top layer has already gone and someone's pinched the orange cream from the bottom'.

Bob blames Terry for his inability to leave the past behind. However, he does not really want to leave it at all – Terry is merely a convenient scapegoat. At the end of the film, in almost the final words of *The Likely Lads*, he tells the apparently departing Terry that 'Without you my life will probably slip into a steady pulse of contentment and happiness.' Terry replies, 'Don't worry kidder, I'll be back to cock it up for you.' It's a fascinating exchange that, in a way, sums up the whole series. To Bob the 'steady pulse of contentment and happiness' is something to be feared; Terry's promise to 'cock it up' is affectionate and what he wants to hear. It's almost as if if Terry didn't exist Bob would have to invent him: he is Bob's rebellion against the certainties of conformity and stability. For all that he loves his wife, for all that he has worked hard to secure a social position, the thought that time has passed him by, that this is all there is from now on, fills him with an unbearable dread.

Ultimately, this is what makes *The Likely Lads* a classic, its willingness to engage with us, laugh with us and feel for us. It is able to do this through the expert way it uses its medium. Ironically, given the great subject of the programme, the most important element in this is

116

'Don't worry kidder, I'll be back to cock it up for you'

time. Television gives us time to develop this relationship and for it to have an effect. This is accentuated in *The Likely Lads* by the two ages of Bob and Terry. When they talk about times past in the 60s, many remember the times they spent with them then too. Their past is our past. The series constantly reminds us of this by echoes of the old age in the revived series, by references in the script, similar situations repeated and jokes reoccurring. 'The Old Magic' reminds us of 'Double Date'; 'Storm in a Tea Chest' is largely a reworking of 'Where Have all the Flowers Gone?', which also inspires sections of 'I'll Never Forget Whatshername'. The ending of the old incarnation in 'Goodbye to All That' is wittily referenced at the end of the film when Terry fails in his plans to leave. All this takes us back; makes us think of 'what became of the people we used to be'.

Coda

The idea of *The Likely Lads* has had a currency long after the series ended. The phrase itself is sometimes referenced in all sorts of ways; a group of Labour MPs who had surprisingly won marginals in the 1997 general election even set up a group called 'The Unlikely Lads and Lasses'. Younger generations respond to the concept too. Ant and Dec, the ubiquitous male chums on British TV screens in the twenty-first century, paid homage to their Geordie roots by appearing in a reworked version of the famous football episode 'No Hiding Place'.[104] They weren't as good, and have stuck to game shows and reality TV since, but their personas and friendship seem to lend itself to doing the lads.

That other tabloid fixture of contemporary Britain, Pete Docherty, also looked to the resonance Bob and Terry have by penning a song with his bandmate in The Libertines, Carl Barât, called 'What Became of the Likely Lads'.[105] This dramatised their tempestuous relationship, revisiting the programme's theme tune in its chorus of, 'Oh what became of the Likely Lads, What became of the dreams we had?'. Docherty and Barât, not even born when the show ended, understood that the reference had an impact, and knew their audience understood that too.

So what did become of the Likely Lads? The last time we see them, Terry is giving his wicked leer on the quayside as Bob sets off accidentally to Bahrain. Dick Clement told me, 'We did talk about doing them again and it's not going to happen and it probably shouldn't happen, but occasionally we thought about what happened afterwards because you do – your characters begin to have a life of their own.'[106] In the early 1990s, Clement and La Frenais publicly suggested that Terry would have come good, having made a pile claiming for an industrial accident, no doubt clasping his thigh in front of the tribunal and then telling them 'I never talk about it'. However, they thought Bob and Thelma would have hit trouble, victims of downsizing and negative equity.[107] What would have happened in the 80s? Would Terry have spent most of it on the dole, like many on Tyneside? Would Bob and Thelma have left the North East, looking for work – moving to, say, Hitchin and working all the hours they could to get that new conservatory? Would they have had children? Is Bob Junior even now worrying about what the folk at the badminton club think?

They would be sixty-four now, nearly retired. Perhaps Bob and Terry still meet on Sunday lunchtime and talk about the old days. I can see them in a corner table, perhaps a bit uncomfortable with each other, passing small talk about their medication and grey hairs and Thelma's dodgy hip. Terry will complain about the euro and Bob will worry about his pension, until conversation comes around to all the conversations they used to have at The Wheatsheaf and The Fat Ox. It's the only thing to look forward to – the past.

Notes

1 From author's interview with Dick Clement, 11 June 2007.

2 Memo from Duncan Wood, 14 July 1964, in BBC files on the programme at Caversham.

3 From author's interview with Clement, op. cit.

4 Ibid.

5 Ibid.

6 BBC Memo from the TV editor of the *Radio Times* to Dick Clement, 16 December 1964.

7 BBC Press Release, December 1964 – in Caversham file.

8 From invoices and memos held at Caversham.

9 Interviews by the author with Clement and with La Frenais, and *Inside Out* (BBC North East tx 6 September 2004).

10 From author's interview with Clement, op. cit.

11 Dates of BBC 2 transmissions of *The Likely Lads*: Series 1 (16 December 1964 to 20 January 1965), Series 2 (16 June 1965 to 21 July 1965), Series 3 (4 June 1966 to 23 July 1966). Dates of repeat transmissions on BBC 1: Series 1 (5 March 1965 to 9 April 1965), Series 2 (23 August 1965 to 27 September 1965), Series 3 (4 October 1966 to 22 November 1966).

12 Commentary from uncredited author of audience research report on first episode, at Caversham.

13 From BBC internal Audience Appreciation Index reports at Caversham.

14 *The Lively Arts*, 'The Unlikely Lads' (BBC 10 October 1976).

15 From author's interview with Clement, op. cit.

16 From author's interview with Ian La Frenais, 22 June 2007.

17 In my interviews with them, Clement and La Frenais talked about the differences in working in film and television. Clement admires the economy required for film and said he now felt some of *The Likely Lads* scenes were a 'little too wordy', although in TV you had to 'create characters that will sustain you'. La Frenais enjoys the 'immediacy' and fast turnaround of TV, compared to film where screenplays 'may not get made or if they do, it's four years from now'.

18 See David Thomson attack on Tony Richardson's work in *Biographical Dictionary of Cinema* (London: Little, Brown, 4th edn, 2002), p. 736.

19 Clement in *The Lively Arts*, op. cit.

20 Clement and La Frenais adapted *Billy Liar* for the stage in the early 70s. Clement told me he loved the book of *Billy Liar* and it was a big inspiration.

21 *The Lively Arts*, op. cit.

22 From author's interview with Clement, op. cit.

23 'Producer' is used as the credit, but in my interview Clement was clear that 'they called it "producer" but it also meant directing'. Clement stayed in touch with all aspects of production however – including being the warm-up man for the studio audience (contracts in the Caversham files).

24 BBC correspondence and memos at Caversham.

25 In his interview with me, Clement explained that they wrote thirteen episodes and were then told to write another thirteen immediately, 'It was like coming down from Everest and being told to go back up again.'

26 *The Sun*, 13 February 1973; *Daily Mail*, 10 January 1973; *Daily Telegraph*, 20 March 1973; *The Guardian*, 4 April 1973.

27 Memo from Duncan Wood to James Gilbert, 10 May 1973.

28 From author's interviews with Clement and La Frenais, op. cit.

29 Various correspondence between BBC and Wright, Webb, Syrett and Son, Richards, Butler and Co. and Elystan Films, 1972–5.

30 From author's interview with La Frenais op. cit.

31 *Omnibus*, 'Whatever Happened to Clement and La Frenais?' (BBC 20 July 1997).

32 *Omnibus*, op. cit.

33 From author's interview with La Frenais, op. cit.

34 Ibid. Clement stated in his interview that 'there is a tyranny of the laugh … I was much happier moving to the hour-long format. I never saw [*Auf Wiedersehen Pet*] as a comedy series.'

35 For instance, in Chris Dunkley's introduction to the BFI TV100 in 2000, <http://www.bfi.org.uk/features/tv/>

36 Andrew Crisell, *An Introductory History of British Broadcasting* (London: Routledge, 1997; 2nd edn, 2002), p. 112.

37 From author's interview with La Frenais, op. cit.

38 Richard Hoggart, *The Uses of Literacy* (London: Chatto and Windus, 1957), p. 33.

39 Although as Lynne Segal notes in her essay 'Look Back in Anger: Men in the Fifties', criticism of patriarchy was slow in developing. See Segal in Jonathan Rutherford and Rowena Chapman (eds), *Male Order: Unwrapping Masculinity* (London: Lawrence and Wishart, 1988; 2nd edn, 1996).

40 Arthur Marwick, *British Society Since 1945* (London: Pelican, 1982), p. 114.

41 Dominic Sandbrook, *White Heat: Britain in the Swinging Sixties* (London: Little, Brown, 2006), p. 572.

42 Marwick, *British Society Since 1945*, p. 162.

43 Edward Heath, the Prime Minister, with his famed festive sense of fun, announced on 13 December 1973 that a three-day week would begin on New Year's Eve. This affected both businesses (including shops) and homes. On 10 February 1974 the National Union of Mineworkers began an all-out strike that added to the energy crisis.

44 In April–May 1966 the trial of the Moors Murderers (Ian Brady and Myra Hindley) took place. Mary Bell was a Tyneside schoolgirl who killed two small boys in 1968. The case re-emerged in 1998, when it emerged that she had been paid for interviews with Gitta Sereny for a book, *Cries Unheard*.

45 See Dave Haslam's book, *Not Abba: The Real Story of the 1970s* (London: Fourth Estate, 2005), for a detailed insight into the full horror of a 70s' theme night.

46 From author's interview with La Frenais, op. cit. Ian went on to explain that as a 'music freak' he had to catch up with punk and the Manchester sound later on.

47 *Whatever Happened to The Likely Lads?* was one of just three or four shows chosen to represent the reality of life in 1973 and portends of the future in a BBC 4 documentary *TV 1973 – The Defining Shows* (tx 6 April 2006).

48 In our interview, Clement claimed that 'there was a practical reason for this – at the time there were very few real Geordie actors … you never used to hear Geordie on TV ever'.

49 *Inside Out*, BBC North East documentary (tx 6 September 2004).

50 From author's interview with La Frenais, op. cit.

121

51 Geoffrey Moorhouse, *Britain in the Sixties: The Other England* (London: Penguin, 1964), p. 14.

52 Ibid., pp. 164–5.

53 Ibid., p. 175.

54 As seen in thinly veiled form in *Our Friends in the North*. The experience of Mary and Tosker in their new flat is a kind of dystopian mirror to Bob and Thelma's new home. See Michael Eaton's BFI TV Classic on *Our Friends in the North* (London: BFI, 2005).

55 Marwick, *British Society Since 1945*, p. 208.

56 Hoggart, *The Uses of Literacy*, p. 93.

57 *The Lively Arts*, op. cit.

58 Ibid.

59 Greg Dyke on *TV 1973 – The Defining Shows*, which included a piece on *Whatever Happened to the Likely Lads?*.

60 Marwick, *British Society Since 1945*, p. 209.

61 Collins details his argument in the book but used this phrase extensively in the accompanying TV documentary, 'The British Working Class', in a series *Class in Britain* (3BM TV/Channel 4, tx 10 July 2005).

62 Hoggart, *The Uses of Literacy*, p. 13

63 From author's interview with Clement, op. cit.

64 From author's interview with La Frenais, op. cit.

65 Norah Vincent, *Self-Made Man* (New York: Viking, London: Atlantic Books, 2006), p. 276.

66 Ibid., p. 273.

67 Mary Ann Doane 'Film and the Masquerade: Theorising the Female Spectator', *Screen* vol. 23 no. 3–4, September–October 1982, pp. 74–87.

68 Eve Kosofsky Sedgwick, *Between Men: English Literature and Male Homosocial Desire* (New York: Colombia University Press, 1985), referenced in Andy Medhurst, p. 120.

69 Medhurst, *A National Joke*, p. 122.

70 Sandbrook, *White Heat*, p. 649.

71 Segal, 'Look Back in Anger', p. 75.

72 Sid Chaplin, *The Day of the Sardine* (London: Eyre and Spottiswode, 1961, republished by Flambards Press, Hexham, 2005), p. 172.

73 From author's interview with La Frenais, op. cit.

74 John Ellis, 'Why does old TV look so weird?', paper at 'Re-Thinking TV History' Conference, King's College, London, 19 April 2007.

75 From author's interview with Clement, op. cit.

76 Clive James, *The Observer*, 11 March 1973.

77 From author's interview with Clement, op. cit.

78 *The Lively Arts*, op. cit.

79 Sandbrook, *White Heat*, p. 463.

80 Vincent, *Self-Made Man*, p. 129.

81 Ibid., p. 213.

82 Rutherford and Chapman, *Male Order*, p. 6.

83 Steve Neale and Frank Krutnik, *Popular Film and Television Comedy* (London: Routledge, 1990), p. 233.

84 Ibid., p. 93.

85 In his interview with the author, Dick Clement said of Forsyth's performance that 'She was very funny – she played it brilliantly.'

86 Rodney Bewes, *A Likely Story* (London: Century, 2005), pp. 216–18.

87 *The Lively Arts*, op. cit.

88 Brett Mills, *Television Sitcom* (London: BFI, 2005), p. 34.

89 Ibid., p. 42.

90 Antony Easthope, *What a Man's Gotta Do* (London: Paladin, 1986), p. 88.

91 Ibid.

92 From author's interviews with Clement and La Frenais, op. cit.

122

93 From author's interview with Clement, op. cit.

94 Gerald Mast, *The Comic Mind: Comedy and the Movies* (New York: Bobbs-Merrill, 1973), p. 339.

95 Robin Nelson at TV Symposium, University of Kent, 1 June 2006.

96 Robin Nelson, ' "Quality Television" *The Sopranos* is the best television drama ever … in my humble opinion', in *Critical Studies in Television vol.* 1 no. 1; Karen Lury in *Interpreting Television* (London: Hodder Arnold, 2005); and Catherine Johnson, 'Negotiating Value and Quality in Television Historiography', in Helen Wheatley (ed.), *Re-Viewing Television History: Critical Issues in Television Historiography* (London and New York: I.B. Tauris, 2007), pp. 55–66.

97 Mast, *The Comic Mind*, p. 341.

98 Howard Jacobson, *Seriously Funny* (London: Viking, 1997), p. 223.

99 Philip Larkin, 'Dockery and Son' (Faber and Faber).

100 The Smiths, 'There is a Light that Never Goes Out' (Morrissey/Marr), from *The Queen is Dead* (Rough Trade, 1986).

101 Chaplin, *The Day of the Sardine*, p. 66.

102 From author's interview with Clement, op. cit.

103 *Omnibus*, op. cit.

104 Transmitted 11 May 2002 (Ginger TV/ITV). Ant was Terry and Dec was Bob.

105 On *The Libertines* (Rough Trade 2004).

106 From author's interview with Clement, op. cit.

107 Ibid. and *Omnibus*, op. cit.

123

Bibliography

Bewes, Rodney, *A Likely Story* (London: Century, 2005).

Chaplin, Sid, *The Day of the Sardine* (London: Eyre and Spottiswode, 1961, republished by Flambards Press, Hexham, 2005).

Collins, Michael, *The Likes of Us* (London: Granta Books, 2004).

Creeber, Glen (ed.), *Tele-Visions* (London: BFI, 2006).

Crisell, Andrew, *An Introductory History of British Broadcasting* (London: Routledge, 1997; 2nd edn, 2002).

Crowther, Bruce and Mike Pinfold, *Bring Me Laughter* (London: Columbus Press, 1987).

Easthope, Antony, *What a Man's Gotta Do* (London: Paladin, 1986).

Eaton, Michael, *Our Friends in the North* (London: BFI, 2005).

Haslam, Dave, *Not Abba: The Real Story of the 1970s* (London: Fourth Estate, 2005).

Hoggart, Richard, *The Uses of Literacy* (London: Chatto and Windus, 1957).

Jacobson, Howard, *Seriously Funny* (London: Viking, 1997).

Johnson, Catherine, 'Negotiating Value and Quality in Television Historiography', in Helen Wheatley (ed.), *Re-Viewing Television History: Critical Issues in Television Historiography* (London and New York: I.B. Tauris, 2007), pp. 55–66.

Lewisohn, Mark, *The Radio Times Guide to TV Comedy* (London: BBC Books, 1998).

Lury, Karen, *Interpreting Television* (London: Hodder Arnold, 2005).

Marwick, Arthur, *British Society Since 1945* (London: Pelican, 1982).

Mast, Gerald, *The Comic Mind: Comedy and the Movies* (New York: Bobbs-Merrill, 1973).

Medhurst, Andy, *A National Joke: Popular Comedy and English Cultural Identities* (London: Routledge, 2007).

Mills, Brett, *Television Sitcom* (London: BFI, 2005).

Moorhouse, Geoffrey, *Britain in the Sixties: The Other England* (London: Penguin, 1964).

Neale, Steve and Frank Krutnik, *Popular Film and Television Comedy* (London: Routledge, 1990).

Newcomb, Horace (ed.), *The Encyclopedia of Television* (Chicago: Fitzroy Dearborn, 2004).

Rutherford, Jonathan and Rowena Chapman (eds), *Male Order: Unwrapping Masculinity* (London: Lawrence and Wishart, 1988; 2nd edn, 1996).

Sandbrook, Dominic, *Never Had it so Good: Britain from Suez to The Beatles* (London: Little, Brown, 2005).

Sandbrook, Dominic, *White Heat: Britain in the Swinging Sixties* (London: Little, Brown, 2006).

Segal, Lynne, 'Look Back in Anger: Men in the Fifties', in Jonathan Rutherford and Rowena Chapman (eds), *Male Order: Unwrapping Masculinity* (London: Lawrence and Wishart, 1988; 2nd edn, 1996).

Thomson, David, *Biographical Dictionary of Cinema* (London: Little, Brown, 4th edn, 2002).

Vincent, Norah, *Self-Made Man* (New York: Viking, London: Atlantic Books, 2006).

Weight, Richard, *Patriots* (London: Pan, 2002).

Wickham, Phil, ' "Suet Puddings and Red Pillar Boxes": English National Identity in *Whatever Happened to the Likely Lads?* and *Steptoe and Son*', MA thesis, University of Westminster, 1996.

Filmography

Get Carter (d. Mike Hodges 1971).

Inside Out (BBC North East 6 September 2004).

The Lively Arts – The Unlikely Lads: Dick Clement and Ian La Frenais (BBC 2 10 October 1976).

Omnibus – Whatever Happened to Clement and La Frenais? (BBC 1 20 July 1997).

Our Friends in the North (BBC 1996).

Credits and Episode Guide

The Likely Lads

written by
Dick Clement
and
Ian La Frenais
produced by
Dick Clement
music by
Ronnie Hazlehurst

regular cast
James Bolam
Terry Collier
Rodney Bewes
Bob Ferris
Sheila Fearn
Audrey
Bartlett Mullins
Cloughy
Donald McKillop
Jack
Olive Milbourne
Mrs Collier

series one
designers
Richard Hunt
Geoff Kirkland
associate producer
Sydney Lotterby

1.1 *Entente Cordiale* (tx 16 December 1964)
Bob and Terry return from their first foreign holiday in Spain. They compete over a girl they had seen from afar who they are convinced is French, when she writes to them and visits Tyneside they discover she is, in fact, Welsh.
Christine Collins
Bettine le Beau
Juan Pickering
Was lost but discovered in the BBC's Treasure Hunt appeal.

1.2 *Double Date* (tx 23 December 1964)
Bob and Terry meet Pat and Deirdre in a café and go on a double date. We see events from both perspectives. Features James Bolam's future wife, Susan Jameson.
Coral Atkins
Deirdre
Susan Jameson
Pat

1.3 *Older Women Are More Experienced* (tx 30 December 1964)
Terry pursues the mature, attractive new manager of the works canteen, divorcee Mrs Windsor. Attempting to woo her, he gets invited to her house but has to do numerous maintenance jobs. Her young teenage daughter returns with her date – Bob.
Sandra Payne
Patricia Shakesby
Yvette Rees
Mrs Windsor

1.4 *The Other Side of the Fence* (tx 6 January 1965)
Bob is seconded to the draughtsman's office and determines to get on. He takes Terry to the social, only to be admonished for taking factory staff. He tells his boss where to stick his drawing board.
Michael Sheard
Nesbit
Richard Moore
Blakey
Anneke Wills

This episode always survived but, unaccountably was left off the first issue of The Likely Lads *on DVD. It is now available and is one of the best episodes from the first series.*

1.5 *Chance of a Lifetime* (tx 13 January 1965)
The lads fall victim to a conman and his daughter who convince them to part with cash for tickets to Australia and a new life. A collection at work to help them on their way is pinched by Blakey, who then falls victim to the conman.
Richard Moore
Blakey
Veronica Lang
Cecile
Barry Linehan
Wally Ralph
LOST.

1.6 *The Suitor* (tx 20 January 1965)
Disapproving of Audrey's hairdresser boyfriend, Terry tries to break them up by getting Bob to take her out. At the pub with the boyfriend, however, Terry discovers he is 'one of the lads'.
George Layton
Mario/Ernie

series two
designers
Geoff Kirkland
Martin Johnson

2.1 *Baby It's Cold Outside* (tx 16 June 1965)

The boys date some visiting nurses, but can't find anywhere to take them. They offer to babysit for Jack and try to pass his house off as their own, but are soon rumbled.

Janet Kelly
June
Kate Storey
Rose
LOST.

2.2 *A Star Is Born* (tx 23 June 1965)
The lads enter a talent competition at a city club. Bob plans to recite 'Albert and the Lion' and Terry proposes a Donovan number. Both chicken out at the last minute.

Richard Moore
Blakey
Dilys Watling
Rhona
LOST, although a copy is believed to be with a private collector.

2.3 *The Talk of the Town* (tx 30 June 1965)
Bob discovers he drunkenly proposed to Helen in public and regrets it. Hearing she wants to get hold of him, he is terrified she is pregnant, a presumption also made by everyone that knows him. When she finally meets him, she confesses she is indeed pregnant but by her sailor fiancé.

Helen Fraser
Helen
LOST.

2.4 *The Last of the Big Spenders* (tx 7 July 1965)
Bob and Terry pull a couple of London salesgirls and promise them a good time. They end up broke as they are taken to a variety of expensive hotspots.

Wanda Ventham
Angela

Wendy Richard
Lyn
Michael Sheard
Nesbit
Roger Brierley
Julian
Pamela Greer
Alister Williamson
Paul Lindley
Elsa Fell
DISCOVERED in BFI's 'Missing Believed Wiped'.

2.5 *Far-away Places* (tx 14 July 1965)
The boys take on part-time jobs to fund a holiday. Terry's work in the supermarket is backbreaking, while Bob's cleaning jobs are all too cushy.

Gay Hamilton
Eva
LOST, although a copy is believed to be with a private collector.

2.6 *Where Have all the Flowers Gone?* (tx 21 July 1965)
The lads attend Terry's cousin's wedding and feel conscious of their age; they fall into reminiscing about times past.
LOST, tragically, as it is easily the best episode of this series. Some scenes are reworked in 'Storm in a Tea Chest'.

series three
This series saw a move from Wednesday night to Saturday night, transmitted on BBC 2.
film cameramen
Elmer Cossey
Ian Stone
film editors
Geoffrey Botterill
Pamela Bosworth
designers
Paul Allen
Alan Hunter-Craig

3.1 *Outward Bound* (tx 4 June 1966)
Looking for free love at a rumoured Beatnik squat, the

boys end up camping, cold and miserable. They meet two girls – and a scout troop that proves hard to shake off.

Nerys Hughes
Valerie
James Cossins
scoutmaster
LOST.

3.2 *Friends and Neighbours* (tx 11 June 1966)
Bob dates Lorna Perrin, a middle-class girl whose snooty parents live next door to Terry's aunt. When his slobbish grandad takes over the house there is uproar from the Perrins at his proletarian antics and Bob is caught in the crossfire.

Wilfred Lawson
Grandad
Angela Lovell
Lorna Perrin
Noel Dyson
Mrs Perrin
Glenn Melvyn
Mr Perrin
LOST.

3.3 *Rocker* (tx 18 June 1966)
Bob buys a motorbike. Attempts to ride leave first him, then Terry in plaster. A number of scenes in hospital are reprised in 'In Harm's Way'.

Carole Mowlam
nurse
Derek Sydney
Mr Stacey
Patti Dalton
Carol
Tex Fuller
Derek Seaton
scooter rider

3.4 *Brief Encounter* (tx 25 June 1966)
Ursula visits the North East from Blackpool. She ends up dating both Bob and Terry, although they are unaware of this. Told largely from her perspective.

127

Isobel Black
Ursula
LOST.

3.5 *The Razor's Edge* (tx 2 July 1966)
Bob is ill and grows a beard. When he is told to shave on his return to work a strike is nearly provoked, Terry's initial militancy fading fast.
Irene Richmond
Mrs Ferris
Donald Gee
Godfrey
Geoffrey Hughes
Podge
Antony Baird
Darby
Vickery Turner
Monica
LOST.

3.6 *Anchors Aweigh* (tx 9 July 1966)
The boys go on a boating holiday in Norfolk and fight over girls. Filmed largely on location.
Rosemary Nichols
Sally West
Glenda Ramsay
Marion
LOST.

3.7 *Love and Marriage* (tx 16 July 1966)
The boys visit Duggie, newly married to Helen, and the club goes on its annual trip to Morecambe.
Derek Newark
Duggie
Helen Fraser
Helen
Frank Cowley
Old Dan
Norman Chappell
Archie
A brilliant episode, one of the programme's darkest, tragically LOST.

3.8 *Goodbye to All That* (tx 23 July 1966)

Bob decides to join the Army and leaves the factory. Missing him, Terry joins up too, only to see Bob discharged for flat feet as he reports for duty.
Alex McDonald
Mr Collier
Barry Stanton
George
Tony Caunter
Irene Richmond
Mrs Ferris
Andrew Robertson
Hugh Walters

Whatever Happened to the Likely Lads?

written by
Dick Clement
and
Ian La Frenais

regular cast
James Bolam
Terry Collier
Rodney Bewes
Bob Ferris
music composed and conducted by
Ronnie Hazlehurst
signature tune written by
Mike Hugg
Ian La Frenais

series one
producer
James Gilbert
designers
Tim Gleeson
Gloria Clayton
Allan Anson
lighting
Robbie Robinson
James Purdie
Richie Richardson
film cameraman
Alan Featherstone
costumes
Roger Reece
make-up
Sylvia Thornton
titles/graphics
Mic Rolph

sound
Trevor Webster
Malcolm Johnson
Lance Andrews

1.1 *Strangers on a Train* (tx 9 January 1973)
©1972. BBC
Bob and Terry run into each other on a train after five years without contact. Bob reveals his engagement and there is a misunderstanding leading to them being stuck in Doncaster, not famed, as we discover, for its Latin quarter. They reflect on how the country has changed.
Brigit Forsyth
Thelma
Deidre Costello
woman on train
James Mellor
steward
Angelique Ashly
stripper in club

1.2 *Home Is the Hero* (tx 16 January 1973)
©1972. BBC
Back in 'toon', Terry is disappointed at the less than enthusiastic welcome from all. He gets his first view of Bob's new Elm Lodge life and reveals he is married. Staying in the new house, Thelma mistakes him for Bob and gets into bed with him.
Brigit Forsyth
Thelma
Sheila Fearn
Audrey
Derek Etchells
Stan

1.3 *Cold Feet* (tx 23 January 1973)
©1972. BBC
Bob has doubts about marriage and talks through his fears with Terry. The bans are read out and we find out Bob's middle name.
Brigit Forsyth
Thelma

128

Sheila Fearn
Audrey
Donald Gee
vicar
John Barrett
verger
Shay Gorman
Roy Denton

1.4 *Moving On* (tx 30 January 1973)
©1972. BBC
Bob takes Terry on a tour of their former haunts – all now knocked down. Terry runs away to Berwick and Bob finds him and takes him home, although is put out when Terry refuses a job he has arranged.
Sheila Fearn
Audrey
Ronald Lacey
Ernie
Effie Morrison
landlady
Elizabeth Lax
secretary
Iain Blair
Hughie

1.5 *I'll Never Forget Whatshername* (tx 6 February 1973)
©1972. BBC
Terry tries to look up old girlfriends but finds they have all moved on – or prefer Bob.
Brigit Forsyth
Thelma
Margaret Nolan
Jackie
Sandra Bryant
Glenys
Norman Mitchell
pub manager
Lorna Wilde
barmaid

1.6 *Birthday Boy* (tx 13 February 1973)
©1972. BBC
No one seems to care about Terry's birthday. Bob and Thelma arrange a surprise party for him but he manages

to inadvertently offend all the guests.
Brigit Forsyth
Thelma
Sandra Downes
Janey
Michael Ralph
Hugh
Christopher Biggins
Podge
Norman Mitchell
barman
Shirley Steedman
Deborah
Elissa Derwent
Clare
Olive Milbourne
Mrs Collier
Brian Grellis
Colin
Stephanie Turner
Mary
Derek Etchells
Stan

1.7 *No Hiding Place* (tx 20 February 1973)
©1972. BBC
Bob and Terry determine not to find out the result of the England football match. Flint pursues them around town; at the hair salon, the pub and even the church. When they turn on the TV that night they find the match was abandoned. One of the most famous episodes, remade in 2002 with Ant and Dec in the lead roles. The original is better!
Sheila Fearn
Audrey
Brian Glover
Flint
Donald Gee
vicar
Corbett Woodall
TV announcer
Lorna Wilde
barmaid
Bernard Douglas
Dallas
Brian Godfrey
Garry

Katy Allan
Rita
Drina Pavlovic
Sonia

1.8 *Guess Who's Coming to Dinner?* (tx 27 February 1973)
©1972. BBC
Terry accompanies Bob and Thelma to dinner at Brenda and Alan's after being accused of being Andy Capp. Class warfare ensues.
Brigit Forsyth
Thelma
Sheila Fearn
Audrey
Olive Milbourne
Mrs Collier
Julian Holloway
Alan Boyle
Jacquie-Ann Carr
Brenda Boyle

1.9 *Storm in a Tea Chest* (tx 6 March 1973)
©1972. BBC
Bob is ordered to remove a tea chest of childhood possessions by Thelma. A tug of war ensues between his past and his future. When the future wins, he comes home to find Thelma's chest of her own childhood objects.
Brigit Forsyth
Thelma
Robert Gillespie
police sergeant
Donald Gee
vicar
Michael Stainton
John Owens
policemen

1.10 *The Old Magic* (tx 13 March 1973)
©1972. BBC
Trying to make up for the fact that he has asked someone else to be his best man, Bob takes Terry out for dinner, where they talk about old conquests. They try to chat up two girls – one of whom turns out to be Thelma's

129

sister, Susan. Terry is installed
as best man.
Anita Carey
Susan Chambers
Brenda Cavendish
Norma
Barbara Ogilvie
Mrs Ferris
Gertan Klauber
waiter

1.11 *Count Down* (tx 20 March
1973)
©1972. BBC
The boys are fitted for wedding
suits and Terry meets Thelma's
dad, Mr Chambers. Wedding
preparations becoming
frenzied.
Brigit Forsyth
Thelma
Bill Owen
George Chambers
Joan Hickson
Mrs Chambers
Robin Parkinson
shop assistant
Anita Carey
Susan Chambers
Lorna Wilde
barmaid

1.12 *Boys' Night In* (tx 27
March 1973)
©1973. BBC
Much to Terry's chagrin, Bob
insists on a quiet stag night
in. Beside himself with
nerves, he ends up ruining a
suit and collapses at an all-
night launderette. Assuming
he is drunk, the police arrest
him.
Robert Gillespie
police sergeant
Michael Stainton
policeman

1.13 *End of an Era* (tx 3 April
1973)
©1973. BBC
The big day. The wedding
takes place and Terry
makes a gracious best man
speech.

Brigit Forsyth
Thelma
Sheila Fearn
Audrey
Bill Owen
George Chambers
Joan Hickson
Mrs Chambers
Anita Carey
Susan Chambers
Barbara Ogilvie
Mrs Ferris
Daphne Heard
Aunt Beattie
Christopher Biggins
usher
April Walker
Jutta

series two
producer
Bernard Thompson
designers
Tim Gleeson
Peter Kindred
John Hurst
(studio) lighting
Jimmy Purdie
film cameraman
Len Newson
film editor
Bill Harris
make-up
Penny Delamar
Les/Lee Smith
costumes
Mary Woods
Michael Burdle
(studio) sound
Richard Partridge
Lance Andrews
Larry Goodson

2.1 *Absent Friends* (tx 1
January 1974)
©1973. BBC
Carries on at the point the
first series left off – with Bob
and Thelma en route to their
ski-ing holiday in Norway.
Terry pursues Susan, leaving
Thelma anxious about her
new home.
Brigit Forsyth
Thelma

Bill Owen
George Chambers
Anita Carey
Susan Chambers
Terry Scully
chauffeur
Constantin De Goguel
hotel porter

2.2 *Heart to Heart* (tx 8
January 1974)
©1973. BBC
Bob returns from honeymoon
in plaster and full of lust
for other women. Terry, by
contrast, is melancholic
over Susan. He and Susan
agree to part and he
immediately starts chasing
other women.
Brigit Forsyth
Thelma
Anita Carey
Susan Chambers
Noel Dyson
Mrs Chambers
Norman Mitchell
Jack
Lorna Wilde
Gloria

2.3 *The Ant and the
Grasshopper* (tx 15 January
1974)
©1973. BBC
The contrasting lives of Bob
and Terry. Terry fails to find a
job, but finds luck at the
bookies.
Brigit Forsyth
Thelma
Jacquie-Ann Carr
Brenda Boyle
Julian Holloway
Alan Boyle
Elizabeth Lax
Wendy
Vicki Michelle
Madelyn
Lorna Wilde
Gloria

2.4 *One for the Road* (tx 22
January 1974)
©1973. BBC

Full of vintage wine, Bob is arrested for drunk driving. At the police station he encounters Terry, arrested for football hooliganism. They hatch a plan to swap samples so Bob does not get banned.

Brigit Forsyth
Thelma
Robert Gillespie
1st police sergeant
James Mellor
PC
Leonard Maguire
Dr McKae
Michael Beint
2nd police sergeant
Norman Mitchell
barman
Gertan Klauber
waiter
Phil McCall
Glaswegian
Brian Vaughan
doorman

2.5 *The Great Race* (tx 5 February 1974)
©1973. BBC
Bob and Terry challenge each other to a bike race to Berwick. They cheat – a lot.
Sheila Fearn
Audrey
Bert Palmer
stationmaster
Roy Pattison
lorry driver
Lorna Wilde
Gloria
Patti Dalton
barmaid
Roger Bourne
Sean Flanagan
Clive Warwick

2.6 *Some Day We'll Laugh about This* (tx 19 February 1974)
©1974. BBC
Terry is caught in flagrante by his mother. Desperately looking for privacy, he offers to do odd jobs while Bob and Thelma are ski-

ing in Scotland. Swayed by the charms of the woman at number 39, he leaves the floorboards up and Bob falls through them. The husband at number 39 gives Bob a black eye.
Brigit Forsyth
Thelma
Sheila Fearn
Audrey
Olive Milbourne
Mrs Collier
Helen Cotterill
Sandra
Anthony Haygarth
milkman

2.7 *In Harm's Way* (tx 26 February 1974)
©1974. BBC
Terry becomes a hospital porter. Seeing Bob in outpatients, he disguises himself and ends up causing Bob further injury, not once but twice.
Brigit Forsyth
Thelma
Elizabeth Lax
Wendy
Claire Nielson
Miss Dixon
Pamela Duncan
Sister Kennedy
Alan Hockey
Vic
Louis Mahoney
Frank
Hilda Barry
old lady
James Garbutt
workman

2.8 *Affairs and Relations* (tx 5 March 1974)
©1973. BBC
Bob and Terry go fishing in Northumberland. They encounter Mr Chambers having an affair with his secretary. Thelma arrives and there are misunderstandings with a barmaid pursuing Terry.
Brigit Forsyth
Thelma
Bill Owen
George Chambers

Carole Ann Ford
Valerie
Ann Hamilton
Beryl Atkins

2.9 *The Expert* (tx 12 March 1974)
©1974. BBC
Thelma has left Bob and Terry advises him on how to win her back. His advice is rubbish.
Brigit Forsyth
Thelma
Juliet Aykroyd
Anthea
Bay White
Mrs Greenlands
Rose Power
neighbour

2.10 *Between Ourselves* (tx 19 March 1974)
©1974. BBC
Terry has been staying with Bob, where his sloth and Bob's cleanliness cause friction. Word gets around about the split.
Brigit Forsyth
Thelma
Sheila Fearn
Audrey
Juliet Aykroyd
Anthea
Elizabeth Day
Vivienne
Nova Llewellyn
Moira

2.11 *The Go-between* (tx 26 March 1974)
©1974. BBC
Attempts to get Bob and Thelma back together intensify. Fed up with the nagging, Terry visits Thelma to plead with her to take him back. They go round to find Bob with his head in the oven – he's cleaning it.
Brigit Forsyth
Thelma
Sheila Fearn
Audrey

131

2.12 *Conduct Unbecoming* (tx 2 April 1974)
©1974. BBC
Terry is in court after fighting with Dougie Scaife. Bob attempts to be peacemaker but ends up fighting Scaife himself, after Terry had made up with him. After Bob's court appearance the lads quarrel and fight – in front of the magistrate. A beautifully structured episode; one of Clement and La Frenais' finest half-hours.
Brigit Forsyth
Thelma
James Cossins
magistrate
Juliet Aykroyd
Anthea
Alun Armstrong
Scaife
Maureen Davis
Janice
Colin Cunningham
2nd magistrate
Robin Scobey
policeman

2.13 *The Shape of Things to Come* (tx 9 April 1974)
©1974. BBC
Terry hears his Great Uncle Jacob has died, to no one's sadness but his. After there is an accident at the crematorium, Bob notices a certain resemblance to the old man, particularly when he meets his put-upon best mate, old Joe Hargeaves. The final episode proper, and brilliant summation of many of its concerns.
Sheila Fearn
Audrey
Olive Milbourne
Mrs Collier
Jack Woolgar
Joe Hargreaves
Eve Pearce
Mrs Hope
Rosalind Bailey
nurse

Olive Mercer
Aunt Rose
Helena McCarthy
Aunt Kitty

The Likely Lads
A Special Christmas Edition
(tx 24 December 1974)
©1974. BBC
signature tune written by
Mike Hugg
Ian La Frenais
costume
Elizabeth Waller
make-up
Susan Rothwell
film cameraman
Len Newson
film editor
Bob Rymer
lighting
Jimmy Purdie
sound
Alan Machin
production assistant
Evan King
designer
Tim Gleeson
producer
Bernard Thompson

Terry passes his driving test and gets a job as a fork-lift truck driver and Bob sports a very neat beard. Sacked after a drunken escapade taking Bob home from the pub in the fork-lift, Terry becomes a cab driver and takes Bob and Thelma to a torrid fancy dress party. As Bob fumbles with Joan of Arc in the back of the cab, Thelma orders Terry to take her home. Stealing the cab to take Joan back, Terry leaves a tell-tale clue from his Captain Hook costume ...
Brigit Forsyth
Thelma
Lilian Verner
Sylvia
Joanna Ross
Andrea
John Crocker
police constable

Norman Mitchell
Jack
John White
man in pub
Betty Bowden
woman in pub

The Likely Lads [feature film]

United Kingdom 1976

directed by
Michael Tuchner
produced by
Aida Young
conceived by
Dick Clement
and
Ian La Frenais
director of photography
Tony Imi
editor
Ralph Sheldon
art director
Robert Jones
music composed by
Mike Hugg
©1976. Anglo-EMI
Productions Ltd
production company
Nat Cohen presents for EMI
Film Distributors Ltd
production executive
Philip Collins
production supervisor
Christopher Sutton
production manager
Donald Toms
assistant director
Kip Gowans
continuity
Renee Glynne
camera operator
Tony White
assistant art director
Tim Hutchinson
costumes
Emma Porteous
make-up
Neville Smallwood
hairdresser
Jan Dorman
soundtrack
'Remember When' lyrics by Ian La Frenais, music by Mike Hugg

sound recordist
Kevin Sutton
dubbing editor
Frank Goulding
dubbing mixer
Trevor Pyke

cast
Rodney Bewes
Bob Ferris
James Bolam
Terry Collier
Brigit Forsyth
Thelma Ferris
Mary Tamm
Christina
Sheila Fearn
Audrey
Zena Walker
Laura
Anulka Dubinska [Dziubinska]
Dawn
Alun Armstrong
milkman
Judy Buxton
Iris
Penny Irving
Sandy

Vicki Michelle
Glenys
Roger Avon
Joe, the landlord
Ronald Lacey
Ernie
Michelle Newell
Alice
Susan Tracy
Edith
Gordon Griffin
Cyril
Edward Wilson
Les
Elizabeth Lax
Bob's secretary
Linda Robson
Marcia
Ian McDiarmid
vicar
Eric Mason
truck driver
Hugh Turner
Mr Chipchase
Christian Rodska
pump attendant
Eddie Silver
fireman

Barbara Elliott
demonstrator
Stephanie Lawrence
demonstrator
Bob Ritchie
passer-by
Jim Rushton
demolition worker
Olga Anthony
boutique saleslady
Alan Snell
taxi driver

production details
Made at EMI Elstree Studios,
England, and on location in
Newcastle and Whitley Bay.
Roman Wall location courtesy
of the National Trust (35mm,
colour by Technicolor)
UK theatrical release by EMI
Film Distributors Ltd in April
1976.
Running time
89 minutes 42 seconds

133

Index

137